lonely planet

POCKET SINGAPORE

Ria de Jong,
Morgan Awyong & Jaclynn Seah

Contents

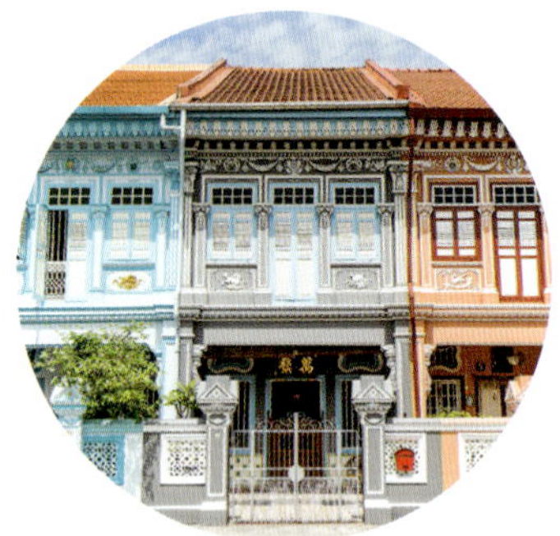

Above: Peranakan terrace houses (p130)
Below: Supertree Grove, Gardens by the Bay (p38)

Plan Your Trip 4

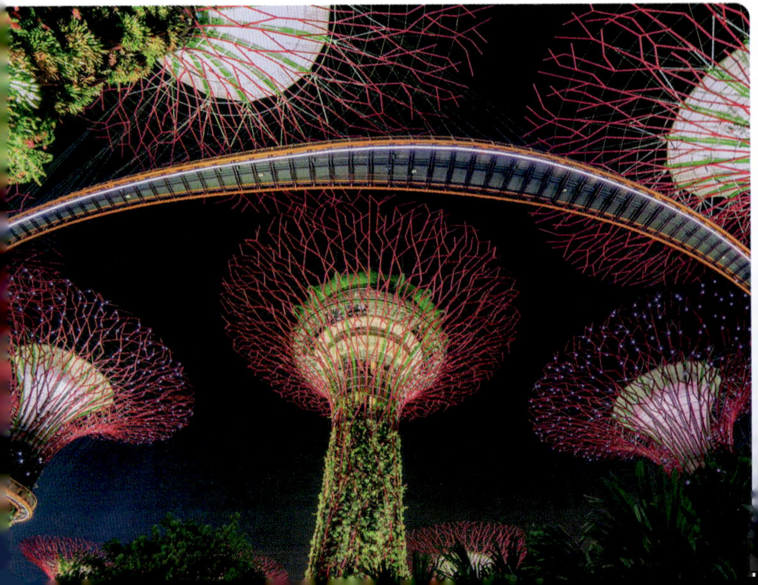

Explore Singapore 33

Singapore Toolkit 175

★ Top Experiences

FROM TOP LEFT: JACK HONG/SHUTTERSTOCK, ZHUKOVA VALENTYNA/SHUTTERSTOCK

The Journey Begins Here

The saying 'good things come in small packages' could have been coined for Singapore. In 2025 the Little Red Dot celebrated 60 years of independence, making now the perfect time to visit. Here, futuristic architecture and effortless efficiency meet lively markets, lush green pockets, smoky temples and pastel-hued heritage shophouses. One moment you're gazing up at a sky garden floating above the city; the next, you're wandering a quiet backstreet steeped in history. And then there's the food – from the creations of celebrity chefs to hawker delights, nothing can quite match the thrill of eating your way across this island. – *by Ria de Jong*

Ria de Jong

@ria_in_transit

Ria is a travel writer and has been based in Southeast Asia for 15 years, 10 of which have been spent on the sunny island of Singapore.

Jaclynn Seah

theoccasionaltraveller.com

Jaclynn is a Singaporean travel writer, tourist guide and occasional traveller perpetually juggling work and wanderlust.

Morgan Awyong

@morgaga

Morgan is a freelance travel writer from Singapore, and can also often be found investigating stories in another city for various global publications.

Jewel Rain Vortex (p133)

L_B_PHOTOGRAPHY/SHUTTERSTOCK

THE BEST

Hawker Centre Experiences

Singapore's hawker culture, integral to its culinary identity, gained UNESCO recognition in 2020. Ensure a visit to at least one hawker centre to fully immerse yourself in the essence of Singapore's vibrant food scene.

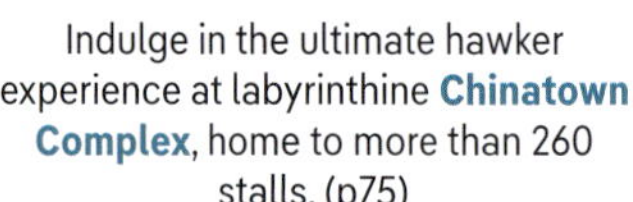

Indulge in the ultimate hawker experience at labyrinthine **Chinatown Complex**, home to more than 260 stalls. (p75)

Duck into **Maxwell Food Centre** (pictured) and witness the legendary queues at its two chicken-rice stalls, renowned for their fierce competition. (p75)

Gorge on some of Singapore's best street eats and Indian food at Little India's heaving **Tekka Centre**. (p83)

Head to perennial lunchtime favourite **Amoy Street Food Centre** to sample some new-gen hawker delights alongside plenty of classics. (p72)

Enjoy the sea breeze as you order up big on satay and seafood at **East Coast Lagoon Food Village** in East Coast Park. (p134)

Save a seat, then wander the open-air courtyard of **Newton Food Centre** (pictured), ringed with 100-plus stalls serving mouth-watering eats. (p108)

Right: Local dishes at Maxwell Food Centre (p75)

FROM LEFT: KAPI NG/SHUTTERSTOCK, NEELAKANDI/SHUTTERSTOCK, KANDL STOCK/SHUTTERSTOCK

THE BEST

Museum & Gallery Experiences

Singapore boasts a plethora of exceptional museums, each bringing to life the island's rich history and evolution, and the captivating tales of its inhabitants.

Delve into the country's history at the **National Museum of Singapore**, the nation's oldest museum and an architectural landmark. (p50)

Travel through time at the **Asian Civilisations Museum**, a tribute to the region's cross-cultural connections. (p46)

Uncover Chinatown's gritty history at the immersive **Chinatown Heritage Centre**, where bygone tales come to life. (p63)

Explore the vibrant Straits Chinese culture through the historical artefacts and immersive displays of the **Peranakan Museum**. (p51)

Learn about the origins and heritage of Singapore's Indian community at the state-of-the-art **Indian Heritage Centre**. (p82)

Immerse yourself in the world-class 19th-century and modern Southeast Asian art at the **National Gallery Singapore**. (p46)

Asian Civilisations Museum (p46)

JACK HONG/SHUTTERSTOCK

MONTICELLO/SHUTTERSTOCK

Sri Veeramakaliamman Temple (p88)

THE BEST

Religious Experiences

Singapore celebrates a variety of faiths, with Buddhism (31%), Christianity (19%), Islam (16%), Taoism (9%) and Hinduism (5%) all commonly practised. Discover this tapestry of religions through the exquisite religious structures found across the island.

Wander through the five-storey **Buddha Tooth Relic Temple**, home to what is reputedly a tooth of the Buddha. (p62)

Discover centuries of tradition and stunning architecture at **Thian Hock Keng Temple** in Chinatown. (p70)

Be enchanted by Kampong Glam's golden-domed **Sultan Mosque**, the stuff of story-book illustrations. (p92)

Soak up the hypnotic energy at **Sri Veeramakaliamman Temple**, Little India's stunning Hindu temple dedicated to the goddess Kali. (p88)

Visit the **Armenian Apostolic Church of St Gregory the Illuminator** and its Memorial Garden, which spotlights Armenians who shaped Singapore. (p52)

THE BEST

WWII Experiences

Singapore's WWII era marked a pivotal chapter in its history, commemorated through various evocative museums and somber wartime sites across the island. They offer poignant insights into this significant period of time.

Experience profound emotions at **Changi Chapel & Museum**, a tribute to the WWII Allied prisoners of war (POWs). (p126)

Head underground to **Battlebox**, the former British command post during WWII, and get lost in the haunting tunnels and chambers. (p53)

Follow Singapore's descent into war at the **Former Ford Factory** and learn about the years of Japanese occupation. (p146)

Learn the story of the Malay Regiment's brave last stand against the Japanese in 1942 at the evocative **Reflections at Bukit Chandu**. (p157)

Visit **Fort Siloso**, Singapore's best-preserved coastal fort on Sentosa Island, for a glimpse into wartime history and the island's military past. (p168)

Cannon, Fort Siloso (p168)

LONGFIN MEDIA/SHUTTERSTOCK

MOTORSPORT PHOTOGRAPHY FI/SHUTTERSTOCK

Singapore F1 Grand Prix (p44)

THE BEST

Nocturnal Experiences

As twilight falls and the air cools, Singapore's vibrant nightlife scene unfolds, catering to varied preferences and desires, and ensuring there's something for everyone to enjoy after dark.

Board the electric shuttles and silently glide past nearly 130 species at acclaimed nocturnal wildlife park **Night Safari**. (p142)

Enjoy jazz tunes and contemporary Singaporean vibes at **Blu Jaz**, one of the best places in town for live music. (p98)

Be seduced by the flavours of Southeast Asia at cocktail den **Native**, which uses locally foraged ingredients. (p76)

Join the party people at raucous **Clarke Quay** to shimmy and shake the night away. (p49)

Lose yourself in Little India's labyrinthine retail giant, **Mustafa Centre**, famed for staying open 24/7. (p88)

Get trackside at the exhilarating **Singapore F1 Grand Prix** night race, roaring around Marina Bay in September/October. (p44)

THE BEST

Foodie Experiences

Food is one of Singapore's greatest drawcards. The nation's melting pot of cultures creates one of the world's most diverse culinary landscapes, just waiting for you to come feasting.

Be awed by Chef Takuya Yamashita's contemporary Japanese spin on classic French cuisine at fine-dining powerhouse **Whitegrass**. (p54)

Chow down at one-dish-only stall **A Noodle Story**, whose Singapore-style ramen is a magnet for local foodies. (p74)

Lick all the way to the bottom of the bowl at cult-status **328 Katong Laksa**. (p129; pictured)

Secure a reservation at **Candlenut** for a decadent meal of refined Peranakan cuisine in a colonial-barrack setting. (p120)

Order some of Singapore's finest *murtabak* (stuffed savoury pancakes; pictured) at **Ar Rahman Royal Prata**. (p96)

In September, join in tastings and cooking workshops at the **Singapore Food Festival**, a celebration of the island's gastronomic heritage. (p24)

Right: Lau Pa Sat (p73)

LIONEL NG/GETTY IMAGES, I AM CONTRIBUTOR/SHUTTERSTOCK, ZAC TAN/LONELY PLANET

SATAY 6

THE BEST

Cocktail Bar Experiences

Once the realm of the iconic Singapore Sling, the city-state has transformed into a global mixology hub, where bartenders experiment with exotic ingredients and innovative techniques in renowned venues and hidden speakeasies.

Savour reimagined classic cocktails with a Singaporean twist at industry veteran **Nutmeg & Clove**. (p56)

Sip a G&T at art deco cocktail lounge **Atlas**, complete with a jaw-dropping 12m-high gin tower. (p99)

Order a tipple inspired by the Golden Age of cocktails at Mad Men–esque **Manhattan**, a must for aficionados of fine libations. (p108)

Experience the forefront of mixology at **Backdrop**, where master bartender Dario Knox introduces percolated cocktails to the world. (p108)

Come join the club at **No Sleep Club** and be wowed by the creations of two Singaporean cocktail legends. (p76)

Step into **Live Twice** and be teleported to 'cinematic' mid-century-modern Japan, complete with razor-sharp, delicious libations. (p76)

Atlas (p99)

TANG YAN SONG/SHUTTERSTOCK

GAIL JOHNSON/SHUTTERSTOCK

Bird Paradise (p143), Mandai Wildlife Reserve

THE BEST

Nature Experiences

Singapore's diverse nature experiences, from tranquil gardens to lush rainforests, exhilarating wildlife encounters and varied hiking trails, offer a serene escape amid urbanity for nature lovers and adventurers alike.

Leap into the future at **Gardens by the Bay**, a land of space-age biodomes, high-tech Supertrees and whimsical sculptures. (p38)

Enjoy a picnic on the **Singapore Botanic Gardens** lawns or wander the ancient rainforest and themed gardens. (p114)

Visit the world-class **Mandai Wildlife Reserve** and get up close and personal with oodles of wildlife. (p142)

Stretch your legs at the **Southern Ridges**, a 10km trail dishing up spectacular nature and city views. (p156)

Tackle the central trail (4km), the most popular section of the 24km trans-island **Rail Corridor** – not for the faint-hearted! (p144)

Spend a day exploring the rustic island of **Pulau Ubin** by bike or on foot. (p127)

THE BEST

Under the Radar Experiences

While Singapore's iconic attractions are undeniably impressive, they offer just a glimpse of local life. To truly discover the essence of this unique island, venture off the beaten path and immerse yourself in its lesser-known treasures.

Dial down the city's frenetic pace at laid-back **Changi Village** (pictured), which offers visitors chilled-out, beachside vibes. (p133)

See Singapore's last remaining dragon kiln at **Thow Kwang Pottery Jungle** and pick up a piece of Peranakan pottery. (p159)

Relax with a soak at **Sembawang Hot Spring** or cook yourself an egg – yes, really! (p147)

Relive your childhood at **MINT**, home to over 50,000 vintage toys from around the world. (p49)

Be amused or terrified at offbeat **Haw Par Villa** (pictured), where quirky sculptures and life-size dioramas depict Chinese ethics and stories. (p154)

Catch a chorus of songbirds perched atop colourful poles at **Kebun Baru Birdsinging Club** on weekend mornings. (p148)

FROM LEFT: ELVIE LINS/SHUTTERSTOCK, SHEE HENG CHONG/SHUTTERSTOCK

Best for Kids

Hop aboard the **Singapore DUCKtours**' brightly coloured remodelled WWII amphibious vehicle for a seriously fun tour of Marina Bay. (p47)

Get up close and personal with plenty of critters at **Mandai Wildlife Reserve**, home to the Singapore Zoo, Night Safari, River Wonders and Bird Paradise. (p142)

Venture to **Sentosa**, Singapore's carefully planned island of fun, boasting a world-class sprawl of theme parks, amusements and beaches. (p163)

Be mesmerised by **Gardens by the Bay**, a futuristic botanical garden with a dedicated Children's Garden featuring wet-play zones and giant tree houses. (p38)

Unveil the wonders of the **Children's Museum**, Singapore's first kid-centric museum (best for under 12-year-olds), with immersive shows and interactive displays. (p51)

Crank up the adrenaline at **Trifecta**, a thrill hub where you can ski, snowboard, skate and surf right on Orchard Rd. (p106)

Best for Free

Marvel at futuristic **Gardens by the Bay** with its high-tech Supertree Grove (and nightly light show), themed gardens and art displays. (p38)

Relive a little 1950s tourism at **Haw Par Villa**, a wonderfully quirky – and more than slightly scary – offbeat theme park. (p154)

Explore the **Singapore City Gallery** to discover the city's evolution from bustling port to high-tech powerhouse, and plans for the future. (p65)

Enjoy one of Singapore's finest views atop the **National Gallery Singapore**. Ascend to the roof of the City Hall Wing to have your breath taken away. (p46)

Spend a morning wandering the **Singapore Botanic Gardens**, a lush oasis featuring diverse flora, serene lakes, art installations and tranquil paths. (p114)

Wander through the streets and alleyways of **Chinatown** to uncover vibrant street art and murals that reveal layers of local culture and stories. (p59)

Perfect Days

DAY ONE

Only Have One Day?

MORNING

Start with a stroll around Marina Bay area, admire the **Marina Bay Sands** (p40) and snap a picture with the **Merlion** (p44; pictured above), before visiting the brilliant **Asian Civilisations Museum** (p46) and **National Museum of Singapore** (p50).

AFTERNOON

Take the MRT to Little India and duck into the **Tekka Centre** (p83) for a smorgasbord of flavour, before exploring the area's colourful history at the **Indian Heritage Centre** (p82). Wander south to Kampong Glam to visit the **Sultan Mosque** (p92) and find unique shops along **Haji La** (p93) and **Arab St** (p93).

EVENING

Head to the futuristic **Gardens by the Bay** (p38) and catch the Garden Rhapsody light-and-sound show.

Sultan Mosque (p92)

FROM LEFT: KADAGAN/SHUTTERSTOCK, MAJONIT/SHUTTERSTOCK, FELIX HUG/SHUTTERSTOCK, DANNY YE/ SHUTTERSTOCK

DAY TWO

A Weekend Trip

MORNING

Head into Chinatown to glimpse neighbourhood life at the **Chinatown Heritage Centre** (p63) and **Thian Hock Keng Temple** (p70; pictured above), before learning all about the metropolis at the **Singapore City Gallery** (p65). Fuel up with some delectable grub at **Maxwell Food Centre** (p75).

AFTERNOON

Dive into Peranakan culture in Joo Chiat, stopping at **shophouses** (p130) on Koon Seng Rd before visiting **Changi Chapel & Museum** (p126). Afterwards, head to the beachfront **East Coast Park** (p132) for a late-afternoon bike ride.

EVENING

Make a beeline for neon-lit **Geylang** (p130), a tame red-light district juxtaposed with temples, mosques and excellent food. Don't miss trying durian at a roadside stall.

DAY THREE

A Short Break

MORNING

Rise early and beat the crowds at **Singapore Zoo** (p142). Grab a 'Park Hopper' combo ticket to visit the other parks at **Mandai Wildlife Reserve** (p142; pictured above). Alternatively, stretch your legs at the verdant **Singapore Botanic Gardens** (p114).

AFTERNOON

Continue the action-packed fun on Sentosa Island. Don your swimmers for thrilling water slides at **Adventure Cove Waterpark** (p171) or, for a mix of rides and shows, tackle **Universal Studios** (p166).

EVENING

Beeline to one of the island's beach clubs for a sundowner before heading back into the city to watch the **Spectra** (p40), a light-and-water show at Marina Bay Sands, before a final satay meal stop at **Lau Pa Sat** (p73).

If You Have More Time

Embark on a morning adventure along the **Southern Ridges** (p156), where panoramic vistas, elevated forest walkways and the pedestrian bridge **Henderson Waves** (p157) await. Visit the poignant war history museum **Reflections at Bukit Chandu** (p157) or the rambling art enclave of **Gillman Barracks** (p157). Conclude your hike with a cable-car ride from **Mt Faber** (p158) to the **VivoCity** (p161) mega-mall, which offers plenty of dining options.

Refuel completed, head to the Technicolour **Haw Par Villa** (p154), an offbeat Chinese mythology theme park that promises a thrilling adventure. Here, those with a strong constitution can brave the frights of Hell's Museum.

Wrap up your day with dinner at Peranakan powerhouse **Candlenut** (p120), a charming dining spot nestled amid the leafy, converted army barracks of **Dempsey Hill** (p118). Then, venture to Chinatown, where lively cocktail dens, including the regionally inspired **Native** (p76) and inventive **No Sleep Club** (p76), serve tempting libations before you hit the dance floors of nearby **Clarke Quay** (p49).

Henderson Waves (p157)

WUTTIPONG POTAWIN/SHUTTERSTOCK

A City Day Trip

Escape to Singapore's 'Far East', just a 30-minute taxi ride from the city centre, for a glimpse of slower, nostalgic local life. Begin a wander through **Changi Village** (p133), to enjoy quaint shops, cafes and colourful street scenes, before boarding a bumboat (motorised sampan) for a short ride to **Pulau Ubin** (p127; pictured above), a rural island hideaway that development has mercifully left behind. Explore its natural wonders, including nature reserves, rustic trails and shrines by foot or bike, remembering to pack plenty of water and sunscreen.

Adventure complete, return to the mainland for a laid-back evening at **Changi Village Hawker Centre** (p134), sampling local delights as the sun sets.

On a Rainy Day

While rain in Singapore is typically brief, seek shelter at either the art-packed **National Gallery Singapore** (p46; pictured above), including the kid-friendly Keppel Centre for Art Education, or delve into Peranakan culture at the nearby **Peranakan Museum** (p51).

Alternatively, explore mall-packed Orchard Rd, offering retail therapy for all budgets, from high-fashion powerhouses **ION Orchard Mall** (p109) and **Paragon** (p109) to high-street-label-heavy **313@Somerset** (p107). You'll also find cinemas, karaoke studios and even an adventure-sports park, **Trifecta** (p106). Plus, there's no shortage of quality food courts, cafes and underground walkways to keep you dry.

Get Prepared

BOOK AHEAD

Six to two months before Book big-ticket events, such as the F1 race, theatre shows or international acts, and secure reservations at must-do top-end restaurants.

One month before Snag tickets to headline attractions and museums, and reserve a table or bar seats at the city hot spots.

One week before Check for local festivals or events and secure a converted Sentosa beach-club daybed.

Manners Matter

Singapore is a conservative and respectful society. Be mindful of not spitting, littering or smoking outside the designated areas when in public spaces. It is also advisable not to show any overt displays of affection and to dress modestly, especially in buildings of worship. Addressing elders as 'uncle' or 'auntie' is a sign of respect and common practice.

How to Hawker

Firstly, save a seat by placing a packet of tissues on each spot you need. Stalls don't typically provide serviettes (napkins), but tissue sellers are usually near the entrance, and sharing tables with strangers is customary. Note your table number, if there is one, as stall owners use it for food delivery. If the stall has a 'self-service' sign, wait for your meal. Return your tray once done – it's required by law.

Things to Know

Clothes Singapore is hot and humid, so lightweight and breathable clothing is a must. Carry a light wrap or sweater if planning on heading indoors, as restaurants and shopping malls are air-conditioned to arctic temperatures.

Skin protection Carry a hat and umbrella to shield you from the sun and rain. Mosquito repellent is a must if heading out into nature, as well as around dawn and dusk.

Chopsticks Avoid spearing food or standing chopsticks upright in rice, as it's rude and unlucky. Don't cross chopsticks or place them on the table; use a chopstick rest or side plate instead.

Strict laws Familiarise yourself with Singapore's laws, which are strictly enforced, from littering and jaywalking to bans on chewing gum and smoking. The death penalty applies for serious offences, including drug trafficking.

TIPPING

Tipping is not customary in Singapore. Most restaurants and hotels include a 10% service charge in the bill; tips at hawker centres are not required. If you had exceptional service, a small tip is appreciated but not obligatory.

Restaurants
10% service charge is added

10%

Bars and pubs
10% service charge is added

Taxis
Round up to the full dollar

Changi Airport
Tipping airport staff is prohibited

DAILY BUDGET

Budget: Less than S$250

- Dorm bed: S$25–50
- Hawker meal: S$4–8
- Ticket to a major museum: S$5–30
- Public transport 24-hour Singapore Tourist Pass: S$17

Midrange: S$250–500

- Double room in a midrange hotel: S$200–350
- Two-course dinner with wine: S$100–150
- Guided tour: S$40–60
- Cocktail at a decent bar: S$25–40

Top End: More than S$500

- Four- or five-star double room: S$500–1500
- Tasting menu in top restaurant: S$350 or more
- Theatre ticket: S$150
- Vespa sidecar tour: S$200 per hour

Currency
Singapore dollar (S$)

Languages
English, Mandarin, Malay and Tamil

Time
Singapore Standard Time (GMT/UTC plus 8 hours)

KYOSHINO/GETTY IMAGES

TIP

Tourists are entitled to claim a refund on the 9% Goods and Services Tax (GST) paid on their purchases made at participating retail stores if they spend more than S$100. See touristrefund.sg.

When to Go

Singapore is an excellent year-round destination, thanks to its warm tropical climate. Rain is frequent but usually brief.

Singapore lacks distinct seasonal variations and has a warm, humid year-round climate. The island experiences almost daily rainfall, but showers are typically short. There are two official monsoons: the northeast monsoon (December to March) and the southwest monsoon (mid-June to September). February to April is the most favourable time to visit, with the lowest rainfall and humidity. The transition months of September and October are also pleasant. From May to August, the haze caused by neighbouring countries' wildfires can affect Singapore.

The Big Events

February: Prepare to be wowed at **Chingay**, Singapore's biggest multicultural street parade, with dazzling floats, colourful costumes and captivating performances that showcase the city-state's diverse talents. Tickets are required.

August/September: Nights come alight for the spectacular **Singapore Night Festival**, as buildings become canvases for rainbow light projections and visitors are treated to interactive installations, performance art and comedy shows.

September: The **Singapore Food Festival** is a culinary extravaganza celebrating the island's rich gastronomic heritage. Local chefs, culinary experts and food enthusiasts come together to enjoy traditional dishes and contemporary creations.

September/October: Marina Bay revs into action with the **Singapore F1 Grand Prix** (p44) night race. Held over three days, it features high-speed action, plenty of glitz and glamour, and big-name entertainment. Tickets sell out quickly, so book well in advance.

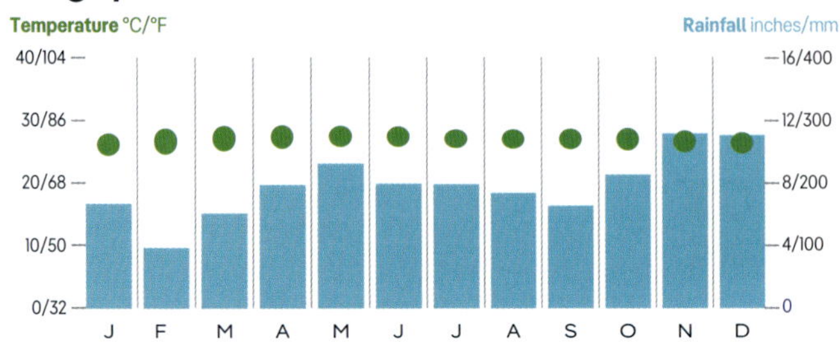

HIT1912/SHUTTERSTOCK

Thaipusam (p89)

Religious Festivities

January/February: The Hindu festival of **Thaipusam** is known for its intense devotion. Amid chanting, music and fervent prayers, pilgrims leave from the Sri Srinivasa Perumal Temple (p89) bearing *kavadis* (heavy metal frames) pierced through their skin.

January/February/March: The streets of Chinatown (p59) come alive with lanterns and lion dancers in the run-up to **Chinese New Year**. Shoppers head to the area en masse to pick up festive treats.

February/March: **Hari Raya**, observed by the island's Muslim community, marks the end of the Ramadan fasting month. After sundown, head to the Geylang Serai Market & Food Centre (p134) or to Kampong Glam (p86) for colourful light decorations and traditional festive treats.

October/November: Little India (p79) is ablaze during **Deepavali**, the 'Festival of Lights', which celebrates the triumph of good over evil with festive lights, fireworks and sweet delicacies. It culminates in a massive street party on the holiday's eve.

ACCOMMODATION LOWDOWN

Singapore ain't cheap, so it's best to avoid the super-peak seasons. School holidays in June and December are busy, as is Chinese New Year. Any large entertainment or sporting event, such as a major concert or the F1 race, will send prices sky-high.

Getting There

Most visitors arrive in Singapore via Changi Airport, 20km northeast of the city centre. Buses and trains also connect Singapore with Malaysia, and ferries connect with Malaysia and Indonesia.

From Changi Airport to the City Centre

By MRT

The Mass Rapid Transit (MRT) is the best low-cost option. The station is located below Terminals 2 and 3. The trip to City Hall costs S$2.14 and takes around 45 minutes. Change trains at Tanah Merah. Trains run between 5.30am and 11.18pm.

By Taxi or Rideshare

Taxi ranks are at all terminals. A trip to the city costs S$25 to S$50, depending on the time of day. Grab rideshare (S$25–35) can be booked via mobile app; there are pickup points at all terminals.

By Bus

Bus 36 runs from Terminals 1, 2 and 3 and from the Carpark 4B bus stop to Colonial District (S$2.26) and Orchard Rd (S$2.32), and takes 75 to 90 minutes. Buses leave every 10 minutes between 6am and 11pm.

By Airport Transfer & Shuttle

Transfers can be booked via the 24-hour Ground Transport Concierges (GTC) counters at all terminals or the Changi app. Private vehicles include four- and six-seaters (S$55/60 per trip to anywhere in Singapore). The City Shuttle is S$5 per person to the Tanah Merah Ferry Terminal; it operates daily from 10am to 7.52pm.

Other Points of Entry

By Land

There are two land-border connections between Singapore and Malaysia; the Johor–Singapore Causeway is the most convenient. From Johor Bahru, buses, taxis and trains are available to cross the border. The **KTM Shuttle Train** *(shuttleonline.ktmb.com.my)* is the fastest, but it terminates just within the border at Woodlands Train Checkpoint. Private bus companies operate services from destinations in Malaysia including Kuala Lumpur, Melaka and Penang.

By Sea

The Tanah Merah Ferry Terminal and HarbourFront Passenger Terminal run services to Malaysia and Indonesia.

Getting Around

Navigating Singapore is a breeze, thanks to its sleek and widespread public transport system which includes an extensive network of trains (MRT) and buses. The city enhances accessibility with bike rentals, affordable taxis and car-sharing options, all supported by plenty of wide, well-maintained footpaths and abundant green spaces.

MRT

Six highly efficient MRT lines crisscross the island. Make sure you remember the name of the last station for the line you're travelling on, as it will help you identify the correct platform for boarding. Also note that MRT stations often have many exits, so look for signs that let you know which letter exit to head to for your destination. Trains operate daily from approximately 5.30am to midnight, with extended hours during festive periods; services run every two to four minutes during peak hours and every five to 12 minutes during off-peak times. A light rail system, **LRT**, connects the MRT with areas further afield.

Bus

Singapore's bus service is modern, safe, affordable and – most importantly – air-conditioned! Designated bus lanes ensure reliable journey times, but expect services during the peak before- and after-work hours to get very busy. Raise your hand to flag down the driver. Tap on with your payment or EZ-Link card and tap off when alighting, or you'll pay the full fare to the end of the line. Bus services, like the trains, run mainly between 5.30am and

FROM LEFT: PORNPRASIT PANADA/SHUTTERSTOCK, TY LIM/SHUTTERSTOCK

ESSENTIAL APP

Download the CityMapper app to plan your journey across various modes of transport.

midnight; however, some run 24 hours a day – for specific timings, check sbstransit.com.sg.

Taxis & Rideshares

If you travel outside peak times, and never in a rainstorm, it's still reasonably affordable to catch a taxi in Singapore. Hailed taxis are metered, or you can lock in a price beforehand via taxi apps CDG Zig or Grab (Singapore's answer to Uber).

Bike Sharing

There are two bike-sharing companies in Singapore: HelloRide and Anywheel. They're relatively easy to use – download the app, set up an account, scan the bike's QR code and get pedalling. Most have GPS tracking to locate designated parking areas; failure to park correctly may incur a S$5 fee. Only foldable bicycles which comply with the allowable dimensions may be brought onto trains and buses.

Walking

Neighbourhoods are best explored on foot, although some of the pavements in Chinatown and Little India are tiny and can get very busy. Keep in mind that the weather can be extremely hot and humid year-round, so opt for cool and breathable clothing. A small umbrella is always a wise choice to shield you from the sun or sudden downpours.

Public Transport Essentials

Travel Fares

If you're in town for more than a day or two, the easiest way to pay for travel on public transport is with the **EZ-Link card** *(ezlink.com.sg)*. The card allows you to travel by MRT trains, local buses, river taxis, the Sentosa Express Monorail and by most taxis. Simply swipe the card over sensors as you enter and leave a station or bus. Another option is to get a one-, two-, three-, four- or five-day **Singapore Tourist Pass** *(thesingaporetouristpass.com.sg)*, which offers unlimited train and bus travel plus perks and discounts at stores and attractions.

Cash is accepted on buses – the correct fare is required, as no change will be provided. Keep the ticket as proof of payment.

Buying Tickets

Paper tickets for public transport are obtainable from ticket machines in MRT stations or directly from bus drivers. The EZ-Link cards, priced at S$10 including a S$5 non-refundable deposit, are available at MRT station customer-service counters and 7-Eleven stores. They can be topped up using cash or cards at station ticket machines.

Alternatively, the Singapore Tourist Pass, starting from S$22 inclusive of a S$10 rental deposit, is available at Singapore Tourist Pass kiosks in Changi Airport and Orchard MRT station, as well as SimplyGo ticket offices in select MRT stations.

How to Pay: EZ-Link vs Bank Card

You can pay for public transport using either an EZ-Link card or a contactless bank card, including those linked to mobile wallets like Apple Pay or Google Pay. Fares are usually the same for both, though EZ-Link cards offer a small discount over single-trip tickets. Note that foreign-issued bank cards may attract a small daily administrative fee.

MRT FINES

Fines apply for eating or drinking, attempting to board a full train, carrying large bags, being intoxicated or lingering for more than two hours.

MRT Etiquette

Singapore's efficient public transport owes much to the mutual respect among commuters. To maintain this harmony, remember to keep to the left when traversing stations (especially on travelators and escalators), queue in designated spots on platforms, allow passengers to alight before boarding, and refrain from pushing. Also, move towards the middle of the carriage to keep doorways clear.

RUCHUDA BOONPLIEN/SHUTTERSTOCK

A Few Surprises

Singapore holds unexpected delights for those willing to explore. Discover remnants of the past, wildlife encounters and hidden treasures.

An Otterly Good Time

Otters have become beloved residents in Singapore, captivating locals and tourists alike with their playful antics. These sleek mammals, primarily the smooth-coated otter, have adapted remarkably well to the urban environment, thriving in the city's waterways and green spaces. Prime otter-family (there are currently 17) sighting spots include the **Marina Bay** (p35), **Gardens by the Bay** (p38) and the Singapore River, showcasing the coexistence of wildlife and urban life in the Lion City. Make sure to keep a safe distance, as otters can be aggressive, and touching or feeding them can result in a hefty fine.

Who Goes There?

As you explore the historic shophouses of **Chinatown** (p59), cast your eyes upwards to view Singapore's original surveillance system. A small section of 2nd-storey flooring was ingeniously made removable, allowing residents to discreetly peep at the bustling five-foot way (roofed passageway in front of shops) below and see who was knocking on their front door!

A Colourful Idea

Lee Kuan Yew, Singapore's founding father and 'chief gardener', orchestrated not only the city's economic and urban transformation but also preserved its greenery. Initiating the Garden City programme in 1967, he adorned overhead pedestrian bridges with bougainvilleas, weaving vibrant **hanging gardens** throughout the cityscape. Head to New Bridge Rd to view some of these bridges in all their bright-pink glory.

OFFBEAT SINGAPORE

Dip your toes, or boil yourself an egg, in the thermal waters of **Sembawang Hot Spring Park** (p147).

Travel back to humbler island days at **Pulau Ubin** (p127), home to one of Singapore's last surviving *kampongs* (villages).

Haw Par Villa (p154) is a theme park of Chinese mythology, with dioramas and the somewhat terrifying Hell's Museum.

Visit Singapore's last dragon kiln at the **Thow Kwang Pottery Jungle** (p159), plus shop a huge range of ceramics.

WHEELSAN IMAGES/SHUTTERSTOCK

***kopitiam* (coffee shop) takeaway coffee**

A Very Special Coffee Culture

Despite Singapore's British colonial history and predominately Asian population, the national drink is not tea but **coffee** – *kopi*, to be precise. Brewed from robusta beans roasted with butter, margarine or even lard, this rich, caramelised coffee is strained through a long flannel sock and poured from a height to create its signature froth. Traditionally served in a china cup and saucer or a tall glass mug, *kopi* fuels the nation, with many Singaporeans drinking several cups a day. Even takeaway has its own local twist, with hawker centres and *kopitiams* (coffee shops) often serving coffee in clear plastic bags tied with string. It is a practical tradition born of thrift and convenience; cheaper than cups, easy to carry and surprisingly good at keeping drinks hot or cold, adding a distinctly Singaporean flair to the daily caffeine fix.

Pee-Yew!

Sometimes, it's not what you see, it's what you smell – and in Singapore, that whiff on the breeze is often the sickly, sweet scent of **durian** (p133) – Asia's king of fruits. You'll spot plenty of 'No Durian' signs banning it from public transport, hotels and shopping malls. If you want to take a sniff yourself, or even a taste (if you dare), head to the Chinatown markets or the streets of local foodie 'hood Geylang where durian sellers will only be too happy to guide you through its famously divisive flavours.

Explore Singapore

Singapore's Walking Tours

Cloud Forest (p38), Gardens by the Bay
AFRIRAMPOE/SHUTTERSTOCK

See p54
for eating, drinking and shopping listings

Explore Downtown & Marina Bay

Researched by Jaclynn Seah

Downtown Singapore is where the city's story began, along the sinuous Singapore River that winds through its heart. Once a maritime trade hub, the quays lined with gritty warehouses are now transformed into vibrant nightlife and dining districts. Nearby, the bustling marketplace has evolved into today's gleaming Central Business District.

North of the river lies the Civic District, its stately buildings echoes of British colonial rule; just beyond in Bras Basah, the former European Quarter is now the city's arts and culture quarter. The river flows into Marina Bay, Singapore's striking modern icon of futuristic architecture built on reclaimed land where the sea once stretched.

Getting Around

MRT

City Hall MRT station serves the Civic District and Marina Bay waterfront. Bayfront Station is connected to Marina Bay Sands and Gardens by the Bay. Clarke Quay Station and Fort Canning Station link the Quays.

Walking

The district is easily walkable and many sights are connected by shaded walkways or underground malls.

Bus

Hop on a public bus for longer connections. Use Google Maps and a contactless credit card for affordable and fuss-free travel around the district.

THE BEST

GARDEN Gardens by the Bay (p38)

ICONIC ARCHITECTURE Marina Bay Sands (p40)

ART GALLERY National Gallery Singapore (p46)

HISTORIC BUILDING Raffles Singapore (p50)

PARK Fort Canning Park (p52)

View of Downtown and Marina Bay

WEERASAK SAEKU/SHUTTERSTOCK

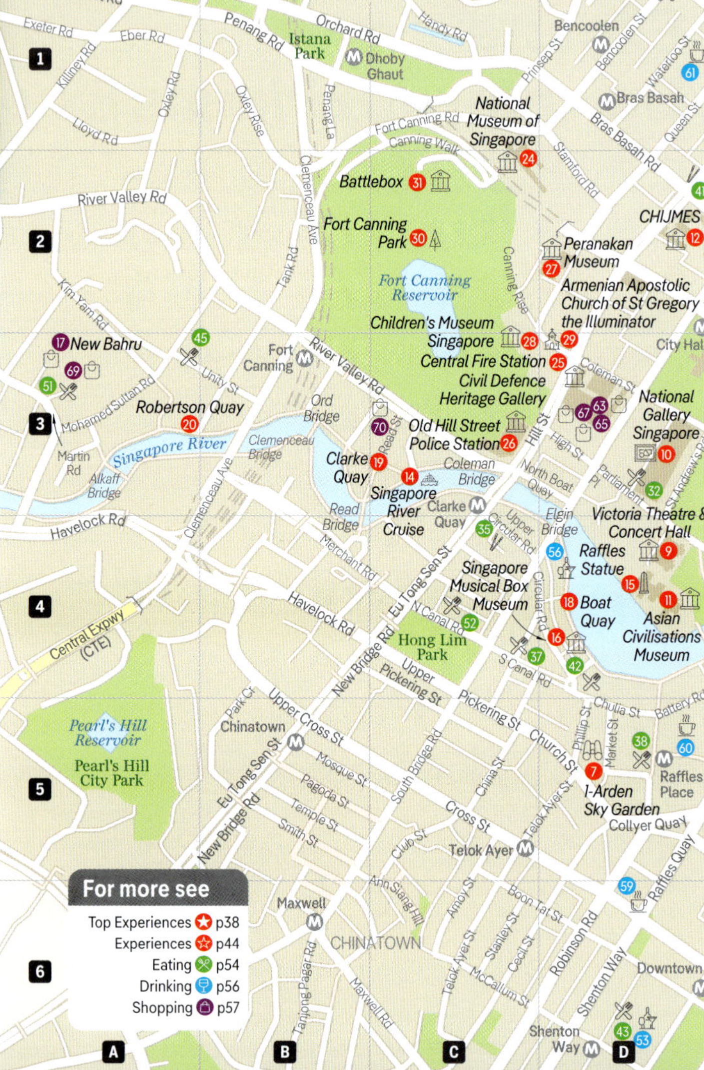
National Museum of Singapore 24
Battlebox 31
Fort Canning Park 30
Fort Canning Reservoir
Peranakan Museum 27
CHIJMES 12
Armenian Apostolic Church of St Gregory the Illuminator 29
Children's Museum Singapore 28
Central Fire Station 25
Civil Defence Heritage Gallery
Old Hill Street Police Station 26
National Gallery Singapore 10
New Bahru 17
Robertson Quay 20
Singapore River
Clarke Quay 19
Singapore River Cruise 14
Victoria Theatre & Concert Hall 9
Raffles Statue 15
Asian Civilisations Museum 11
Boat Quay 18
Singapore Musical Box Museum 16
Hong Lim Park
Pearl's Hill Reservoir
Pearl's Hill City Park
Chinatown
CHINATOWN
I-Arden Sky Garden 7
Istana Park
Dhoby Ghaut
Bencoolen
Bras Basah
City Hall
Fort Canning
Clarke Quay
Raffles Place
Telok Ayer
Maxwell
Downtown
Shenton Way
For more see
Top Experiences p38
Experiences p44
Eating p54
Drinking p56
Shopping p57

E
F
G
H
1
2
3
4
5
6
Bugis
0 500 m
0 0.25 miles
Middle Rd
Victoria St
North Bridge Rd
Rochor Rd
Ophir Rd
Nicoll Hwy
Republic Ave
Bain St
MINT
Cashin St
Purvis St
Seah St
Beach Rd
Long Bar
Singapore DUCKtours
Raffles Singapore
Bras Basah Rd
Esplanade
Rochor Rd
Temasek Ave
Temasek Blvd
Republic Blvd
East Coast Pkwy (ECP)
Promenade
Civilian War Memorial Park
Stamford Rd
Raffles Link
Raffles Blvd
Padang
Connaught Dr
Esplanade Dr
Esplanade – Theatres on the Bay
Raffles Ave
Esplanade Park
Singapore Flyer
East Coast Pkwy (ECP)
Esplanade Bridge
Jubilee Bridge
Anderson Bridge
Merlion Park
Helix Bridge
Cavenagh Bridge
Fullerton Rd
Merlion
Marina Bay
ArtScience Museum
One Fullerton
SkyPark Observation Deck
Satay by the Bay (350m); Marina Barrage (550m)
Marguerite
Collyer Quay
Fullerton Bay Hotel
Clifford Pier
Spectra
Lantern
Marina Bay Sands
Gardens by the Bay
Bayfront
Dragonfly Lake
Bayfront Ave
Marina View
Straits View
Sheares Ave
Marina Blvd
Marina Gardens Dr
MARINA SOUTH
Central Blvd

★ TOP EXPERIENCE

Gardens by the Bay

Welcome to the botanic gardens of the future, a fantasy land of space-age bio-domes, high-tech Supertrees and whimsical sculptures. This visionary oasis, spanning 101 hectares of reclaimed land in the city's heart, is a triumph of urban planning that thrills architecture lovers and nature enthusiasts alike.

MAP P36 **H5**

PLANNING TIP
Visit in late afternoon or early evening, when the heat softens and the Supertrees burst into colour during the nightly sound-and-light show **Garden Rhapsody**, at 7.45pm and 8.45pm.

Scan this QR code for full opening hours and to book ahead.

The Conservatories

Housing 217,000 plants from 800 species, the Gardens' asymmetrical **conservatories** *(gardensbythebay.com.sg; adult/child S$46/32 for both biodomes)* rise like giant paper nautilus shells beside Marina Bay. The **Flower Dome** holds the Guinness World Record for the largest glass greenhouse, occupying an area equivalent to 75 Olympic-size swimming pools. The innovative megastructure replicates a dry Mediterranean climate, maintaining a temperature of 23°C to 25°C. Free tours run every weekend from 2pm to 5pm.

Recreating the tropical montane climate found between 1500m and 3000m altitude, the **Cloud Forest** houses one of the world's tallest indoor waterfalls and a lush mountain clad with plants from around the world. Feel the spray of the 35m-high waterfall, stroll the aerial **Cloud Walk** and look out for carnivorous Venus flytraps, delicate blue oil ferns and mosses.

Supertree Grove

The majestic Supertrees are the centerpiece of Gardens by the Bay, their bionic-like branches soaring skywards like a canopy from a sci-fi realm. Adorned with 162,900 plants from over 200 species, these steel-clad concrete structures act as vertical gardens. Seven of the 18 Supertrees also generate solar power used to light and cool the conservatories.

RUSLANKPHOTO/SHUTTERSTOCK

It's free to roam around the grove and watch the **Garden Rhapsody** light-and-sound show that takes place every night at 7.45pm and 8.45pm. Fifty metres up on top of the highest Supertree is the **Supertree Observatory** *(adult/child S$14/10)* where you can drink in the views of Singapore's cityscape from the rooftop deck. For more thrills, walk across the 22m-high **OCBC Skyway** *(adult/child S$14/10)* bridge suspended amid six Supertrees.

QUICK BREAK
Fine-dine inside the Flower Dome at Michelin-starred **Marguerite**. For a cheaper feed, opt for alfresco hawker centre **Satay by the Bay**.

Marina Barrage

Singaporean ingenuity in action, **Marina Barrage** *(pub.gov.sg)* is both a flood-control dam of the Marina Channel and a gorgeous park with commanding skyline views. The curvaceous strip of lawn atop the building is popular with Singaporean families and kite enthusiasts, particularly at sunset.

The on-site **Sustainable Singapore Gallery** *(free)* includes fascinating archival footage of the Singapore River before its extreme makeover and a nifty working model of the Marina Barrage itself.

★ TOP EXPERIENCE

Marina Bay Sands

Since its 2010 opening, Marina Bay Sands has become the symbol of Singapore. Designed by Israeli-born architect Moshe Safdie, the Integrated Complex consists of three 55-storey hotel towers fronted by an exhibition hall, shopping mall and museum along with a theatre and a casino.

MAP P36 **F5**

PLANNING TIP
Visit on a weekday to avoid the crowds. The SkyPark is particularly crowded just before sunset so give yourself enough time to queue for the lift.

Scan this QR code for opening hours and to book tickets.

Skypark Observation Deck

The 1.2-hectare **SkyPark Observation Deck** *(marinabaysands.com; adult/child from S$35/31)* floats 56 floors up atop the hotel's three iconic towers like a massive grounded ship. While its internationally famous infinity pool is just for hotel guests, the observation deck is open to the public and offers dramatic vistas across the Singapore skyline.

Sunset is the most popular time to visit. Hang around to see the city lights come on after dark for a different view. To enjoy views with proper seating, go to rooftop restaurant **CÉ LA VI** (see p56) on level 57. The S$38 cover charge includes one drink and guests are limited to the restaurant premises.

Spectra

Every night, the waterfront of Marina Bay Sands razzle-dazzles with a free water-and-light show, **Spectra** *(8pm & 9pm daily, also 10pm Fri & Sat)*. The 15-minute extravaganza features dancing fountain jets, video projections and laser displays, backed by an orchestral soundtrack.

You can catch Spectra from the water on the **Singapore River Cruise** (p47) on selected boats half an hour before showtime. If you want to watch two light shows in one evening, start with the 8pm Spectra show at Marina Bay Sands, and then cut

PINGLABEL/SHUTTERSTOCK

through the hotel via the overpass to Gardens by the Bay in time to see Garden Rhapsody at 8.45pm.

ArtScience Museum

Fronting Marina Bay is the **ArtScience Museum** *(pictured; 10am-7pm Sun-Thu, to 9pm Fri & Sat)* looking like a giant white lotus framed by a lily pond. With 21 galleries spread over three storeys (mostly underground), the venue houses exhibitions that push the boundaries of science and technology. A must-visit is the permanent exhibition **teamLab Future World** *(adult/child from S$35/29)*, created by renowned Japanese digital-art collective teamLab, where visitors are immersed in interactive light art exhibits with nature and floral themes. The interactive walls where hand-drawn sketches are digitally scanned and come alive on the wall are particularly popular with children.

QUICK BREAK
Rasapura Masters near the ArtScience Museum at the Shoppes Basement 2 offers a wide variety of affordable food and drink options.

Walk the Civic District

Immersed in history and culture, the Civic District is a captivating blend of iconic landmarks. Stroll through streets adorned with architectural marvels and explore the city's top museums and galleries. Along the riverbanks, witness the narrative of Singapore's evolution.

START	END	LENGTH
Raffles Singapore	National Gallery Singapore	2.4km; 2½hr

Cathedral of the Good Shepherd
Fort Canning Park
Fort Canning Reservoir
Queen St
Victoria St
Canning Rise
Armenian St
Bras Basah Rd
Beach Rd
START
Esplanade
Nicoll Hwy
Stamford Rd
City Hall
Armenian Apostolic Church of St Gregory the Illuminator
Children's Museum Singapore
Civilian War Memorial Park
Raffles Blvd
Central Fire Station
Coleman St
North Bridge Rd
St Andrew's Rd
Hill St
Old Hill Street Police Station
River Valley Rd
High St
Padang
Raffles Ave
Esplanade Dr
END
Coleman Bridge
North Boat Quay
Parliament Pl
Clarke Quay
Elgin Bridge
Old Parliament House
Esplanade Park
Parliament House
Eu Tong Sen St
New Bridge Rd
Raffles Statue
Victoria Theatre & Concert Hall
Esplanade Bridge
Empress Pl
Asian Civilisations Museum
Anderson Bridge
Marina Bay
South Bridge Rd
Singapore River
Cavenagh Bridge
Hong Lim Park
0 200 m
0 0.1 miles

1 A Grand Old Dame

Marvel at the splendour of the **Raffles Singapore** (p50) facade from the palm-studded driveway along Beach Rd. Then wander the hotel's lush tropical gardens and charming shopping arcade before emerging onto North Bridge Rd.

2 Prayers to Parties

Head left and cross Bras Basah Rd to reach **CHIJMES** (p47), a former convent transformed into an entertainment hub. The Gothic chapel, where the wedding scene from the 2018 blockbuster movie Crazy Rich Asians was filmed, is now a popular party venue. Opposite stands the Cathedral of the Good Shepherd, Singapore's oldest Roman Catholic church.

3 Peranakan Perfection

Continue south along Victoria St, crossing Stamford Rd. Turn right and follow Stamford Rd until you reach the pedestrian boulevard of Armenian St, with various museums including the must-visit **Peranakan Museum** (p51). Follow the street, then turn left onto Coleman St where you'll pass the **Children's Museum Singapore** (p51) and the **Armenian Apostolic Church of St Gregory the Illuminator** (p52), Singapore's oldest church.

4 Colourful Facades

Turn right into Hill St, home to two architectural gems. Firstly, you'll encounter the striking red-and-white brick facade of the **Central Fire Station** (p51), housing the **Civil Defence Heritage Gallery**. Further on, admire the vibrant rainbow shutters adorning the neo-Renaissance **Old Hill Street Police Station** (p51).

5 A River Stroll

Turn left to stroll the northern bank of the **Singapore River**. This is Boat Quay, one of the finest vantage points to admire the CBD's towering skyscrapers, which contrast with the historic shophouses along the riverbanks. You'll pass landmarks such as **Parliament House** and the **Raffles statue** (p48), marking the supposed British landing point in Singapore, along the way.

6 Architectural Giants

Explore the remarkable architecture of the neo-Palladian **Asian Civilisations Museum** (p46), and the iconic **Victoria Theatre & Concert Hall** (p45) – one of Singapore's earliest examples of Victorian Revivalist design – and the **Old Parliament House**, Singapore's oldest surviving government building.

7 Knockout Art with a View

Stroll north along St Andrew's Rd to reach the City Hall and Old Supreme Court, the stately buildings now housing the **National Gallery Singapore** (p46). Make your way to the 6th floor for a panoramic view of the city skyline.

EXPERIENCES

Snap the Merlion, a Mystical Maritime Mascot

STATUE

MAP: 1 P36 **E4**

In the 1960s, the imaginative minds at the tourism board spun a captivating tale, giving rise to the iconic symbol of Singapore: the **Merlion**. Overlooking Marina Bay and spouting water from its mouth, this majestic 8.6m-high statue's fish-like body symbolises Singapore's origins as a fishing village, while its leonine head honours the city's original name, Singapura, which means 'lion city' in Sanskrit. Drawing plenty of snap-happy tourists, the Merlion stands guard at the mouth of the Singapore River facing east – an auspicious feng shui orientation believed to bring prosperity (which, looking at the Singapore skyline, it certainly has done).

Visit Singapore's Original Port of Entry at Clifford Pier

LANDMARK

Strolling the waterfront opposite Marina Bay, you can experience the city's swanky side at **One Fullerton** (MAP: 2 P36 **E4**; *fullertonhotels.com*), where a stretch of elegant bars and restaurants beckon. Beyond them stands **Clifford Pier** (MAP: 3 P36 **E5**), originally a landing point for immigrants and seafarers. The pier was easily recognised by the red oil-lamp beacons that shone at night as a warning to ships – locals came to call it *ang theng* ('red-lamp pier' in Hokkien). Today, while its exterior is largely unchanged, Clifford Pier's interior has been converted into a sophisticated restaurant that forms part of the **Fullerton Bay Hotel** (MAP: 4 P36 **E5**) which pays homage to the pier's heritage.

Enjoy Waterfront Performances at the Esplanade

ARTS CENTRE

MAP: 5 P36 **E3**

On the northern bank of Marina Bay, the spiky domes of the **Esplanade – Theatres on the Bay** *(esplanade.com)* house a 1800-seat concert hall, a 1940-seat theatre and an outdoor stage. Curious visitors can take guided tours to learn more about the architecture and take a peek at what goes on backstage. The centre organises plenty of free events around its complex, including annual cultural festivals, art exhibitions, indie film screenings and music gigs. The outdoor theatre with the backdrop of Marina Bay waterfront is particularly picturesque in the evenings no matter what's on stage. Find updates and book tickets online, or visit the box office on the mezzanine level.

Zip Along the F1 Street Race Route

ANNUAL EVENT

Since 2008, Singapore has hosted the annual **Singapore F1 Grand Prix** *(singaporegp.sg)*, the first Formula One night race created to avoid the city's sweltering afternoons. The 300-plus-kilometre circuit winds through the streets of Marina Bay, zipping past landmarks like the National Gallery Singapore, the war memorial Cenotaph and even the usually pedestrian-only Anderson Bridge. For most of the year the route looks like any other road, but things change in early September when barriers go up, lights are installed and grandstands rise – preparations begin as early as a month before race week. Swing by the Pit Building near the Singapore Flyer; it's closed unless hosting events, but the painted pit lane makes for fun photos.

Get a Bird's-Eye View from the Singapore Flyer

OBSERVATION WHEEL

MAP: 6 P36 **H3**

A half-hour ride aboard the 165m-high **Singapore Flyer** *(singaporeflyer.com; adult/child S$40/25)* offers a million-dollar panorama over the island from its location on the Marina Promenade. On a clear day, views from this Ferris wheel stretch from the high-rise housing sprawl in the east to the shipping docks in the west, with Indonesia visible beyond the ship-filled expanse of the South China Sea. Sunset and weekends are when the Flyer is busiest. You can also enjoy a four-course dinner in the privacy of your own capsule with the Sky Dining experience.

BEST MARINA BAY VIEWPOINTS

Sky-high spots around Marina Bay offer great aerial views of Downtown.

1-Arden Sky Garden

MAP: 7 P36 **D5**

Lush gardens amid sleek architecture on the roof of CapitaSpring, 51 storeys up. Book slots online at 1-arden.sg. 8.30-10.30am, 2.30-5.30pm & 6-10pm

Level 33

Slurp house-brewed beer at 'the world's highest urban craft brewery' (p56) 33 storeys high in the Marina Bay Financial District. noon-11pm

Lantern

MAP: 8 P36 **E5**

Not particularly lofty but with an excellent waterfront location atop the Fullerton Bay Hotel. 3pm-1am Sun-Thu, to 2am Fri & Sat

Catch Performances at Victoria Theatre & Concert Hall

PERFORMING ARTS VENUE

MAP: 9 P36 **D4**

Enjoy concerts, recitals and music performances at Singapore's oldest performing arts venue. The regal **Victoria Theatre & Concert Hall** *(artshouselimited.sg/vtvch)* consists of three structures. The oldest is the theatre section which began as the Town Hall in 1862, while the 600-seat concert hall was added in 1902 to commemorate Queen Victoria's passing. Completed a few years later is the 54m-high Clock Tower linking the two buildings.

Stand in the atrium and observe the two distinctly different architectural styles between the theatre and concert hall on either side. Adventurous folk can sign up for the Clock Tower Climb *(S$50)*, a tour where you ascend rickety ladders for a closer look at the five bells that chime the familiar Westminster tune hourly at the top of the tower. You must be 18 or older to join the tour.

Admire the Art at the National Gallery

ART GALLERY

MAP: 10 P36 **D3**

The **National Gallery Singapore** *(nationalgallery.sg; adult/child S$20/15)* occupies the beautifully restored former City Hall and Old Supreme Court buildings. It houses the world's largest public collection of Southeast Asian modern art of over 8000 artworks within two national monuments connected by a striking aluminium and glass canopy.

Permanent exhibition 'Between Declarations and Dreams' showcases 300 artworks that trace the art history of Southeast Asia from the mid-19th century. Those travelling with kids shouldn't miss the gallery's Keppel Centre for Art Education, where kids are encouraged to interact with artworks and create their own masterpieces. There are various themed guided tours held regularly; the Back-of-House tour takes you to parts of the Old Supreme Court that are usually out of bounds to the public.

Much of the National Gallery premises is free to explore, though the exhibitions and tours require a gallery pass; prebook online or buy tickets at the Coleman Street & Padang Visitor Services Counters on Level 1.

Trace History at the Asian Civilisations Museum

MUSEUM

MAP: 11 P36 **D4**

Perched beside the Singapore River, the **Asian Civilisations Museum** *(nhb.gov.sg/acm; adult/child/under-6s S$25/20/free)* is both an ethnographic museum and an art gallery showcasing the history of Asian peoples and cultures. Its remarkably curated galleries, spread over three levels, are home to Southeast Asia's most comprehensive collection of pan-Asian treasures. Of note is the 9th-century Tang Shipwreck collection. This sunken vessel, lost off the coast of Sumatra a millennium ago, was laden with over 60,000 Tang dynasty ceramics among other treasures, offering insights into the history of regional trade.

Have a Night Out at CHIJMES

NIGHTLIFE HUB

MAP: 12 P36 **D2**

CHIJMES *(chijmes.com.sg)*, pronounced 'chimes', is a historic complex now housing heaving bars with live music and upscale restaurants. It's open to the public and free to visit – wander through its beautiful fountain-lit courtyards and admire the intricately designed metal staircases and stained-glass windows designed by the renowned Irish architect George Coleman.

Dating back to 1854, the building was originally a convent school named CHIJ (Convent of the Holy Infant Jesus), established by an order of French Catholic nuns. CHIJMES Hall was the former Gothic chapel, though now it's a venue for parties and weddings, most notably featured in the 2018 movie *Crazy Rich Asians*. The main building after you enter the complex, Caldwell House, is one of the oldest surviving buildings in Singapore. The other buildings play host to restaurants and live-music bars.

Take Like a Duck to Water with DUCKtours

BOAT TOUR

MAP: 13 P36 **F2**

Embark on the delightfully quirky **Singapore DUCKtours** *(bigducktours.com; adult/child S$53/43)*, a one-hour adventure aboard the *Wacky Duck*, a remodelled WWII amphibious Vietnamese war craft. The route traverses land and water, with a focus on Marina Bay and the Colonial District. Tours depart hourly from 10am to 6pm from Suntec City. They are informative, loud and over the top, especially when the vehicle ventures off-road into Marina Bay!

Sail the Singapore River

BOAT TOUR

MAP: 14 P36 **C3**

The **Singapore River Cruise** *(rivercruise.com.sg; adult/child S$28/18)* is an easy way to explore the downtown area without too

LAWN OF LEGACY

The large green field amid the many conserved colonial-era buildings in the Civic District may appear unassuming, but the **Padang** (Malay for 'field'; Map p36 E3) is steeped in Singapore's history. One of the oldest public recreation grounds, this expansive field has witnessed pivotal events from the jubilant victory parade after Japan's WWII surrender in 1945 to celebrations marking Singapore's merger in 1963. Gazetted as a National Monument in 2021, the Padang today hosts regular sporting events – it's home to the Singapore Cricket Club and Singapore Recreation Club – as well as Singapore's National Day Parade during milestone years.

much effort. A 40-minute ride on a bumboat (motorised sampan) that used to transport goods along the river will take you from Clarke Quay jetty through Boat Quay and make a loop around Marina Bay before returning to Clarke Quay. Sit in the open-air section at the back of the boat for the best views. Queues form around sunset and in the evenings when temperatures are cooler.

Book online or at the Clarke Quay jetty; pay extra if you'd like to catch the Marina Bay Sands' Spectra (p40) light show from the water *(adult/child S$42/28)*; boat departures are at 7.30pm and 8.30pm, half an hour before the show.

Hunt the Original Raffles Statue

STATUE

MAP: 15 P36 **D4**

Most people snap a shot with the white marble **statue** of Singapore's British founder Sir Stamford Raffles, standing prominently along the Singapore River near the Asian Civilisations Museum. It supposedly marks the landing site of the British when they arrived in Singapore in 1819.

But walk towards the entrance of the Victoria Theatre & Concert Hall (p45), and you'll find the same statue, only in bronze, standing beneath the Clock Tower. This is the original Raffles statue that locals nicknamed *Orang Besi* ('iron man' in Malay) and was installed on Jubilee Day in 1887, predating the white marble statue which was unveiled in 1972.

Listen to History at the Singapore Musical Box Museum

MUSEUM

MAP: 16 P36 **D4**

The **Singapore Musical Box Museum** *(singaporemusicalbox museum.org; adult/child S$20/12)* showcases a private collection of more than 40 antique music boxes, some dating back over 200 years. You'll see everything from early, simple mechanisms to cupboard-sized marvels packed with multiple instruments – one was even meant for the *Titanic* but never made the voyage. The museum also highlights Singapore's lesser-known link to the craft, with local artisans once trained to make and repair these intricate machines; look out for the rare Singapore-made piece on display. Guided tours last about an hour, and reservations are essential – email ahead to check availability.

Get Creative at New Bahru

LIFESTYLE HUB

MAP: 17 P36 **A3**

A short walk from dining district Robertson Quay, **New Bahru** *(newbahru.com)* – Bahru also means 'new' in Malay – is a trendy lifestyle destination occupying the restored grounds of the former Nan Chiau High School. Heritage meets hip in this creative cluster, with old classrooms and hallways in the peachy orange complex now housing over 40 homegrown brands, from local fashion labels to skilled craftspeople, perfect for picking up a made-in-Singapore keepsake.

Highlight venues include **MAKE by Ginlee** *(makestudio.sg)*, where visitors can customise their own bags with the brand's signature pleats; **Crafune** *(crafune.com)* workshops to craft your own leather accessories; and **Woods in the Books** *(woodsinthebooks.sg)*, a local bookstore that specialises in picture books.

To get here, take the MRT to Fort Canning Station on the Downtown Line or the free shuttle bus every 30 minutes (11am to 9pm) from Pan Pacific Suites Orchard along Somerset Rd.

Revisit Childhood Faves at the MINT

MUSEUM

MAP: 21 P36 E2

MINT *(emint.com; adult/child S$30/20)* may be a Museum of Toys, but it's really designed for nostalgic parents rather than kids – in fact, MINT actually stands for Moment of Imagination and Nostalgia with Toys. Founded by toy collector Chang Yang Fa in 2007, this four-storey building houses his personal collection of more than 50,000 items (around 8000 of which are on display). The toys hail from 40 countries and date as far back as the 1840s; they run the gamut from rare *Flash Gordon* comics to original Mickey Mouse dolls. Beyond the toys, the permanent collection includes two galleries devoted to vintage enamel signs.

QUAYS OF THE SINGAPORE RIVER

Once central to Singapore's bustling entrepôt trade, the historic quays along the Singapore River have reinvented themselves as lively nightlife districts, each with its own distinct vibe.

Boat Quay

MAP: 18 P36 D4

The conserved *godowns* (warehouses) house a mix of alfresco restaurants and cosy bars popular with the nearby office crowd.

Clarke Quay

MAP: 19 P36 C3

Painted in rainbow hues and pedestrianised, this bustling precinct is brimming with nightclubs and restaurants along the waterfront promenade.

Robertson Quay

MAP: 20 P36 A3

Calmest of the quays, this district favoured by expats has plenty of riverside eateries, cafes and galleries, perfect for leisurely meals and strolls.

Consider paying a little extra for the 'Around the World in 60 Minutes' guided tour to get more context to the displays. There's also a small gift shop selling replica tin toys and old-school games. The museum is closed on Monday.

Time-Travel Through Raffles Hotel HOTEL

Raffles Singapore (MAP: 22 P36 **E2**; *raffles.com*) may reserve its opulent lobby for hotel guests, but it's still well worth a visit for its elegant ivory facade, famous Sikh doorman and lush tropical courtyards. What began as a modest beachfront bungalow in 1887 (before land reclamation pushed the shoreline far away) quickly grew into a symbol of colonial-era luxury and remains one of Singapore's most iconic hotels to stay in.

Its most famous draw is the **Long Bar** (MAP: 23 P36 **E2**), birthplace of the Singapore Sling in 1915, where visitors still line up to sip the classic pink cocktail and toss their peanut shells on the floor like the good ol' days, or pop by the Raffles Boutique (p57) to pick up Sling-related souvenirs and other Raffles paraphernalia.

Dive into Singapore's Past at the National Museum MUSEUM

MAP: 24 P36 **C2**

It might be the nation's oldest museum – dating back to 1887 – but there's nothing stuffy about the **National Museum of Singapore** *(nhb gov.sg/nationalmuseum; adult/child S$24/18)*. Underneath its 19th-century colonial exterior is a high-tech institute that uses cutting-edge multimedia to take you on a journey through Singapore's short but action-packed history.

The permanent exhibition **Singapore History Gallery** on Level 1 charts six centuries of development from the settlement's founding as Singapura, through its role as a Crown colony to its occupation in WWII. It's temporarily closed for upgrading until October 2026. The Glass Rotunda

BEHIND THE SINGAPORE SLING

The **Long Bar** at Raffles Hotel is where bartender Ngiam Tong Boon crafted the Singapore Sling in 1915. At the time, it was deemed improper for women to publicly consume alcohol, relegating them to juices and teas. Recognising an opportunity, Ngiam devised a cocktail that resembled juice but concealed an alcoholic kick. The original gin-based concoction features pineapple and lime juice, Cointreau, Benedictine and Angostura Bitters, with grenadine and cherry liqueur imparting its pink hue, though the current recipe has seen some tweaks. A Sling at the Long Bar will set you back S$44.

on Level 2 presents **Singapore Odyssea: A Journey Through Time**, an immersive multimedia experience. An RFID wristband pairs you with a digital native animal companion that guides you through Singapore's evolving seascape and regional legends.

Get Snap-Happy on Hill Street

ARCHITECTURE

Hill Street, along the southern foot of Fort Canning Park, offers some of Singapore's most photogenic architecture. The 1909 **Central Fire Station** (MAP: 25 P36 D3) stands out with its striking red-and-white 'blood-and-bandage' facade. Still an active fire station and a national monument, it also houses the **Civil Defence Heritage Gallery** *(scdf.gov.sg)*, where antique fire engines and hands-on firefighting exhibits draw families and history buffs alike.

A short stroll away, the **Old Hill Street Police Station** (MAP: 26 P36 C3) captivates with its grid of rainbow-coloured shutters. Completed in 1934 as one of the largest police stations in Malaya with more than 280 living quarters, it was notoriously used as an interrogation centre during the Japanese occupation. Today, it serves as a government office and remains a favourite Instagram backdrop along the Singapore River.

Explore Singapore's Heritage at the Peranakan Museum

MUSEUM

MAP: 27 P36 D2

Visit the **Peranakan Museum** *(nhb gov.sg/peranakanmuseum; adult/child S$18/12)* to explore the rich heritage of the Peranakans – people of mixed Chinese and Malay/Indonesian heritage, largely descendants of Chinese traders who married local Malay women. Inside a classic Straits Settlements bungalow on the pedestrianised Armenian St, the museum has the world's finest collection of Peranakan artefacts, spread out in 10 permanent galleries across three floors.

Highlights include the variety of decorative textiles that Peranakan women were known to painstakingly embroider and hand bead, as well as all the intricate colourful dining porcelain on display on the installation of a *tok panjang*, a traditional long dinner table typical of Peranakan households. Open 10am to 7pm Saturday to Thursday; to 9pm on Friday.

Take the Kids to the Children's Museum

MUSEUM

MAP: 28 P36 C3

It may be small but the **Children's Museum Singapore** *(heritage.sg/childrensmuseum;adult/child S$17/11)* is the first museum in Singapore dedicated to visitors aged under 12. It's housed in a former primary school built over a century ago along Armenian St. Don't miss the **Hidden Chamber**, an immersive theatre show in which the captain opens his secret stash of treasure and shares stories about its origins. Tiny tots (aged two to four) can join the **Play Pod**, a fun area for free play, while older kids can explore the **Maze of Amazement**. The museum is closed on Monday; there are four fixed time slots for entry – 9am, 11am, 2pm and 4pm.

See Singapore's Oldest Church

CHURCH

MAP: 29 P36 **D3**

As you stroll along Armenian St, you can't miss checking out the eponymous **Armenian Apostolic Church of St Gregory the Illuminator** *(armeniansinasia.org)*. Consecrated in 1836, this is the oldest church in Singapore designed by its pioneer colonial-era architect, George Coleman. The Armenians were the first Christian community to build a permanent place of worship in Singapore. The Memorial Garden highlights notable Armenians in Singapore's history, including Agnes Joaquim, who hybridised Singapore's national flower (the Vanda Miss Joaquim orchid), and the Sarkies brothers, who built the Raffles Singapore hotel. The church is free to visit.

Walk in the Kings' Footsteps at Fort Canning Park

PARK

MAP: 30 P36 **C2**

The hill occupied by **Fort Canning Park** *(nparks.gov.sg)* has over time served as the royal grounds of 14th-century Malay kings, the seat of British colonial power and a key site of Singapore's WWII fight. Today, Fort Canning's lush trails, archaeological sites and preserved structures showcase Singapore's transformation over the centuries.

Nine themed gardens can be found on its grounds – the **Artisan's Garden** is one of Singapore's few archaeological dig sites where researchers have found evidence of an ancient artisan's workshop. The

THE FALL OF SINGAPORE

The Battle of Singapore (8 to 15 February 1942) was a critical engagement during WWII that culminated in the fall of the British stronghold. Japanese forces, commanded by General Tomoyuki Yamashita, executed a meticulously planned invasion, exploiting weaknesses in the British strategy. Despite being deemed an impregnable fortress, Singapore succumbed in a mere seven days. The surrender of more than 80,000 Allied troops marked the largest capitulation in British military history. The fall of Singapore had profound geopolitical implications, shattering the perception of imperial invincibility and reshaping the dynamics of power in the Pacific. It accelerated the Japanese advances and started Japan's regional dominance.

TANG YAN SONG/SHUTTERSTOCK

grounds of the **Spice Garden** were once part of the British rulers' attempt at a botanical garden and showcase the cash crops they tried to grow like nutmeg and cloves. The **Fort Canning Heritage Gallery** (pictured) on top of the hill offers excellent context to the history of the fort and respite from all that walking.

Descend into WWII Past at the Battlebox

MUSEUM

MAP: 31 P36 **C2**

During the Battle of Singapore in WWII, Fort Canning's hilltop Far East Command Centre was where the decision to surrender Singapore to the Japanese was made on 15 February 1942. It's now known as **Battlebox** *(battlebox.sg)*. Take an audio tour and descend almost 9m underground into the bomb-proof bunker. Wander the eerie maze filled with life-size mannequins and dioramas recreating the morning when Singapore fell to invading forces. Admission is free but bookings are required. The enhanced experience *(adult/child S$20/15)* gives access to two 270-degree projection rooms for a truly immersive experience of this pivotal historical moment.

Best Places for...

See p36 for map of locations

$ Budget $$ Midrange $$$ Top End

Eating

Fine Dining

Odette $$$

32 D3
Timeless French fine dining guided by the seasons, crafted by triple-Michelin-starred chef Julien Royer. *6.30-8.15pm Mon, noon-1.15pm & 6.30-8.15pm Tue-Sat*

Whitegrass $$$
see 12 D2
Chef Takuya Yamashita blends classic French cuisine with a contemporary Japanese spin, creating a refreshingly innovative culinary experience. *noon-2.30pm & 6-10.30pm Tue-Sat*

Waku Ghin $$$
33 F5
The exquisiteness of the 10-course modern Japanese-European degustation menu by acclaimed chef Tetsuya Wakuda is nothing short of breathtaking. Reservations are a must. *5-11pm*

Summer Pavilion $$$

34 G3
The epitome of Cantonese culinary excellence, where traditional dishes are elevated with contemporary flair. From delicate dim sum to sumptuous seafood, each dish is a masterpiece. *11.30am-2.30pm & 6.30-10.30pm*

Soups & Noodles

Song Fa Bak Kut Teh $
35 C4
This cult-status *bak kut teh* is a soothing concoction of melt-in-the-mouth pork ribs simmered in a peppery broth of herbs, spices and whole garlic cloves. *11am-9.45pm*

LiXin Teochew Fishball Noodles $
36 E2
A beloved eatery that's been delighting diners with its authentic Teochew flavours, handmade fishballs and flavourful noodles since 1968, offering a taste of tradition in every bite. *10am-9pm*

Hock Lam Beef $

37 C4
Fourth-generation noodle stall serving silky *kway teow* with tender beef slices in rich gravy, topped with salted vegetables and crushed peanuts. *10.30am-8pm Mon-Fri, 10am-6.45pm Sat & Sun*

City Hot Pot $$

38 D5
This cult favourite hot-pot restaurant serves up individual pots and set meals with 16 soup bases to choose from; perfect for solo travellers and those who dislike sharing. *11.30am-3pm & 5-10pm*

Dumplings & Dim Sum

Victor's Kitchen $$
39 D1
Cosy Hong Kong–style dim sum eatery known for its delicious oozing egg-yolk custard buns and chilled milk tea (no ice to dilute!) *10.30am-8pm Sun-Thu, to 9pm Fri & Sat*

Madame Fan $$$

40 E2
Swoon over traditionally prepared dim sum elevated with contempo-

rary ingredients. The Dim Sum Drink Sum weekend brunch is legendary. 11.30am-2.30pm & 6-10pm Mon-Fri, 11.30am-3pm & 6-10pm Sat & Sun

Wah Lok $$$

 D2

A favourite among locals for special-occasion meals, this Cantonese classic serves one of Singapore's best dim sum lunches. Book ahead for weekends. *11.30am-2.30pm & 6.30-10pm Mon-Sat, from 11am Sun*

Burgers & Pizzas

Wild Child Pizzette $$

 D4

The slow-fermented bases at this minimalistic pizzeria are heavenly light and airy. The toppings send you into another taste stratosphere. *11.45am-2.30pm & 6-10pm*

d.o.c $$

 D6

Helmed by a professional pizzaiolo, pizzas here are wood-fired using applewood, giving a layer of sweetness. Expect perfection. *11am-11pm*

Black Tap Craft Burgers & Beers $$

 F5

If you have an appetite, these extra-juicy burgers will hit the spot; if you're famished, wash it down with one of the crazy milkshakes. *11.30am-11pm Mon-Fri, from 11am Sat & Sun*

WILD/FIRE $$

 A3

Clad in soft brioche buns, these perfectly charred stone-axe Wagyu burgers can be a bit of a messy handful, but they are so worth it. *hours vary*

Free-Flow Buffets

Colony $$$

 G3

Dine at what's touted as the ritziest buffet in town – the seafood spread is legendary. Sunday's Vintage Champagne Brunch elevates it up another notch. *6.30-10.30am, noon-2pm & 6-10.30pm Mon-Sat, noon-3.30pm & 6-10.30pm Sun*

Edge $$

 F3

Come hungry to this legendary hotel buffet featuring seven bustling kitchens that span Singaporean, Indian, Japanese and Cantonese cuisines. *6.30-10.30am, noon-2.30pm & 6-10pm Mon-Fri, to 3pm Sat & Sun*

Lavo $$$

 G5

Experience lively Sunday vibes at this Italian eatery's Champagne Brunch, with DJs setting the mood as you indulge 57 storeys high amid Singapore's stunning skyline. *noon-midnight*

Tess Bar & Kitchen $$

 E2

Offering a Boozey Brunch Buffet (you can forgo the booze) on weekends, this industrial-chic shophouse serves Asian-influenced European fare. *4pm-1am Mon-Thu, to 3am Fri, noon-3am Sat, noon-1am Sun*

Breakfast & Brunch

YY Kafei Dian $

50 E2

Old-school *kopitiam* (coffee shop) for home-style Hainanese fare like the soft toasted *kaya* buns. *7.30am-7pm Mon-Fri, from 8am Sat & Sun*

Common Man Coffee Roasters $$

51 A3

This airy, industrial-cool cafe is Singapore's go-to spot for all-day brekkie winners. The menu is simple yet inspired, and bonus: they roast and serve top-class coffee. *7.30am-6pm*

Punch $$

 C4

In this minimalist cafe with a stunning courtyard, the menu may seem simple yet each breakfast offering

looks delicious, making decisions a delightful challenge. *8am-6pm*

Glasshouse $$

see 12 D2

Minimalist cafe at CHIJMES whose all-day breakfast menu brims with classics such as bagels and salmon tartines. Save room for a delectable sweet pastry. *8am-10pm*

Drinking

Rooftop Bars

Cook & Brew

53 D6

This chic gastro-bar atop Westin Singapore has lofty views, an extensive drinks menu and happy hour till 10.30pm most evenings. *hours vary Mon-Sat*

Level 33

54 E6

Laying claim to being the world's highest 'urban craft brewery', Level 33 brews lager, pale ale, stout, porter and wheat beer – order the tasting paddle to try them all. *noon-11pm*

CÉ LA VI

55 G5

Perched on Marina Bay Sands' SkyPark, this bar offers a smack-yourself-in-the-face panorama of the Singapore skyline. The S$38 cover charge is redeemable for food or drinks. *hours vary*

Southbridge

56 D4

Rising above the glut of mediocre Boat Quay bars, this discerning rooftop bar delivers a stunning skyline and river vista. Go for the fresh oysters. *5pm-midnight*

Cocktail Dens

Last Word

see 57 E2

This sleek bar behind the Japanese curtain is dedicated to reviving your passion for classic cocktails. With an emphasis on precision and fresh produce, expect the unexpected. *5pm-midnight*

Nutmeg & Clove

57 E2

Shifting from its original Chinatown location, this industry veteran expertly reinterprets classic cocktails with a Singaporean twist. *5pm-midnight*

Writers Bar

see 22 E2

Want the Raffles experience but not the Long Bar's super-sweet Singapore Sling? Head to this refined cocktail den discreetly located in the Grand Lobby. *5-11pm Mon-Thu, to 11.30pm Fri & Sat, noon-3pm & 5-11pm Sun*

MO Bar

58 F3

Located in the Mandarin Oriental, this swanky hotel bar oozes class and crafted cocktails. The themed evenings from Monday to Wednesday always pull a crowd. *5pm-midnight Sun-Thu, to 1am Fri & Sat*

Coffee Stops

Alchemist

59 D6

This frill-free coffee spot delivers robust brews with a no-fuss approach. It's mainly grab-and-go customers but there are a few benches if you'd like to linger. *8am-5pm Mon-Fri*

Wai Cafe

60 D5

Brightly coloured business-district cafe offering vintage feels and a delightful caffeine fix served in charming takeaway cups, perfect for a quick pick-me-up. *8am-5.30pm Mon-Fri*

Kurasu

61 D1

While the cafe's aesthetics lean towards minimalism, its coffee is anything but. Select from specialty roasts sourced from across Japan; the staff will happily help you choose. *10am-6pm*

Narrative Coffee Stand

 E2

A nook in the Bras Basah Complex for those who love their espresso and pour-overs. *8am-5pm Mon-Fri, from 9am Sat & Sun*

Shopping

Lifestyle Boutiques

Green Collective SG

63 D3

Step into a sustainable haven at this multibrand collective, offering a treasure trove of zero-waste essentials from cutlery kits to jewellery, fashion and accessories. *11am-9pm*

Raffles Boutique

 E2

It might sound like a tourist trap, but Raffles Boutique has a curated selection of exquisite products, predominantly with a Singapore theme, alongside branded Raffles souvenirs and giftware. *10am-8pm*

Barehands Loft @ Funan

 D3

This local fashion brand with a social cause works with various artisans from around Asia including marginalised communities and refugees to tailor-make their laidback looks. *11am-9pm*

Singaporean Finds

Supermama

see 11 D4

A gallery-esque store brimming with contemporary giftware, including Singapore-inspired pieces crafted by local designers. The blue-and-white fine-porcelain dishes made in Japan are the headliners. *10am-7pm Sat-Thu, to 9pm Fri*

When I Was Four

 E2

Embrace the local charm at this design studio offering a playful twist on everyday items, from Singapore-inspired tees to quirky leopard-balm socks. *noon-7pm Mon-Fri, 12.30-6.30pm Sat*

Love, Bonito

 D3

This homegrown fashion brand founded by Singaporean Rachel Lim is a firm favourite among local women seeking functional, versatile and well-made garments. *11am-10pm*

TWG Tea Boutique

 E2

Singapore's posh tea purveyor sells more than 800 single-estate teas and blends sourced globally, from English breakfast to Rolls Royce varieties like 24-carat-gold-coated Grand Golden Yin Zhen. *10am-10pm*

Niche Interests

MORNING

 A3

Flagship store for local coffee-tech company MORNING's coffee-tasting events and capsule-machine demos. *hours vary*

Swee Lee Clarke Quay

70 C3

A music-lover's dream with music retail, vinyl listening stations and live music, along with a chill cafe and bar. *11am-9pm*

Basheer Graphic Books

 E2

A cosy bookstore stocked from floor to ceiling with all kinds of graphic books, from fashion titles to architecture-themed coffee-table tomes. *10am-8pm Mon-Sat, 11am-7pm Sun*

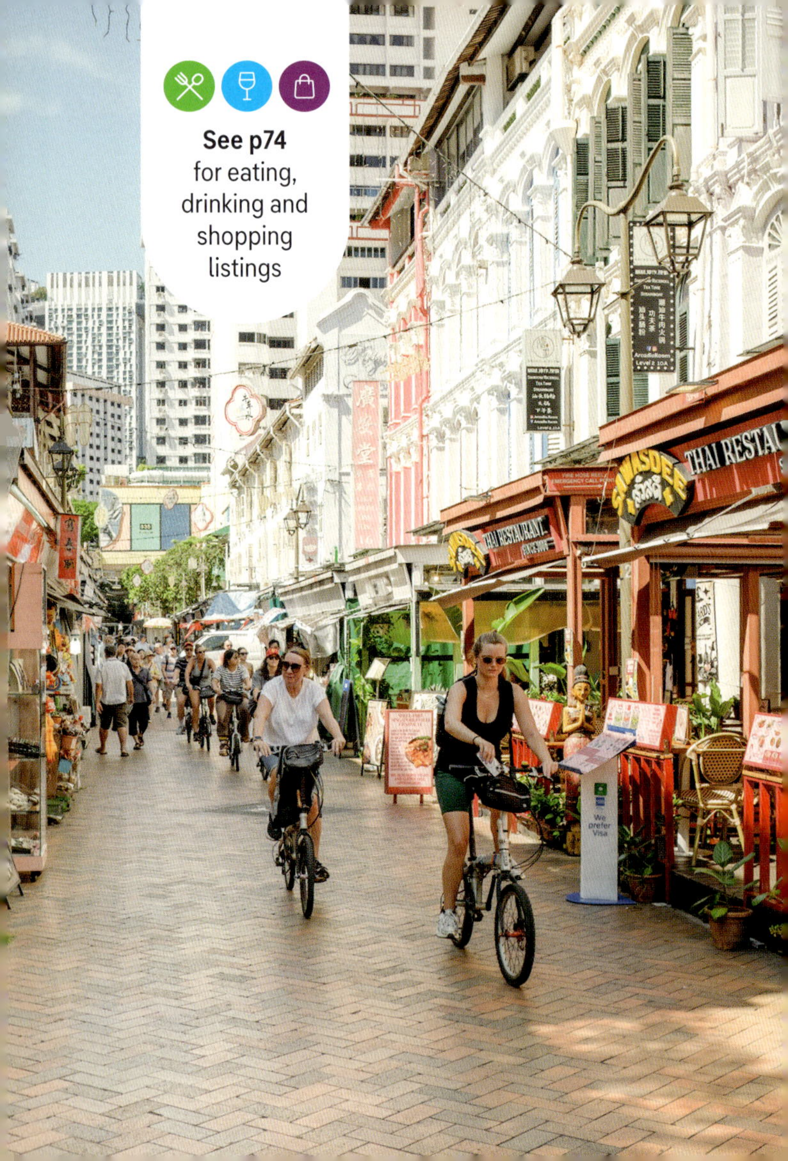

See p74 for eating, drinking and shopping listings

Researched by Morgan Awyong

Explore Chinatown & the CBD

When British administrator Stamford Raffles carved up Singapore on ethnic lines, Chinese settlers were allocated land west of the Singapore River. Life in colonial Chinatown was tough, characterised by cramped quarters and harsh work. And despite the district's name, the earliest inhabitants included Malay and Indian brethren, as evidenced by the mosques and Indian temples along the streets. Today, heritage shophouses sit beside shiny skyscrapers. Gone are the clattering rickshaws and makeshift street-food stalls, replaced by efficient public transport, organised hawkers and vibrant street art. The area still awakens early, bustling with wet markets and *kopitiams* (coffee shops). Evenings remain lively with hip bars, trendy restaurants and late-night LGBTIQ+ haunts.

Getting Around

MRT

Well-served by three MRT lines, Chinatown station is at the heart of the neighbourhood. Pick Telok Ayer station for the array of eateries and bars towards the CBD, or Maxwell for exploration of southern spots.

Walking

Pavements are easily traversable, and numerous shophouses offer pleasant shade with their narrow five-foot ways (covered verandahs offering shelter).

Bicycle

While hilly at parts, the neighbourhood is easily explorable on wheels. Keep a lookout for traffic as there are no dedicated cycling paths and some roads are narrow.

THE BEST

TEMPLE Buddha Tooth Relic Temple (p62)

MUSEUM Chinatown Heritage Centre (p63)

PERANAKAN HERITAGE Baba House (p64)

HAWKER CENTRE Amoy Street Food Centre (p72)

GALLERY Singapore City Gallery (p65)

Chinatown (p66)
18042011/SHUTTERSTOCK

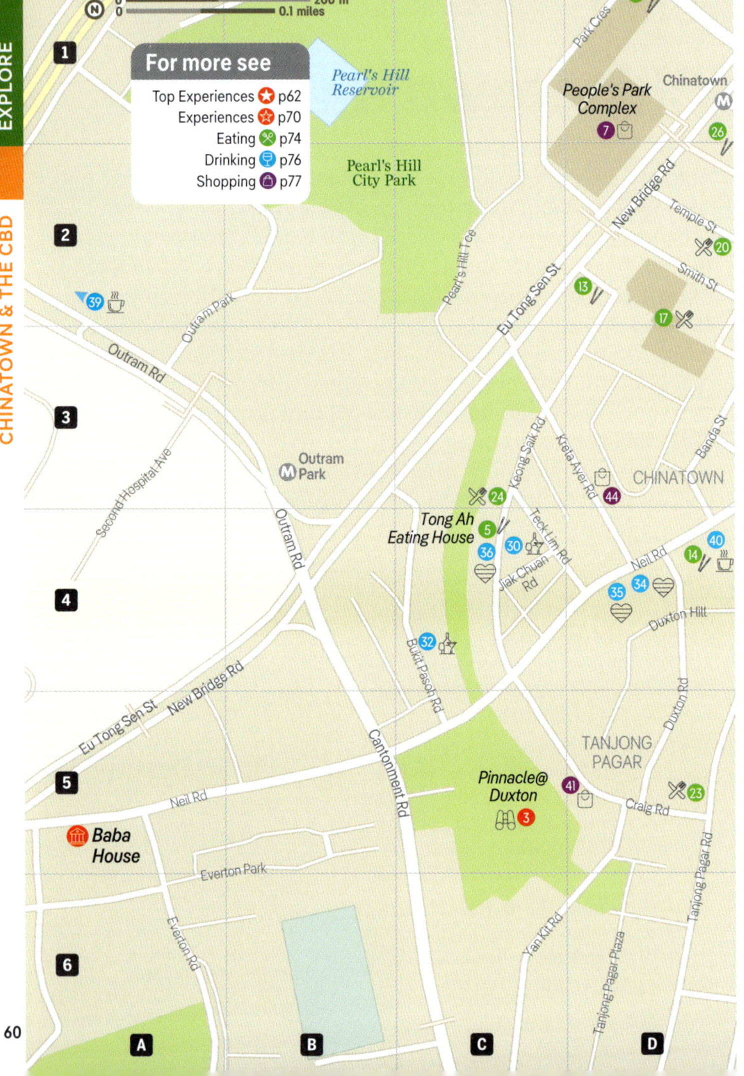
A
B
C
D
1
2
3
4
5
6
0 200 m
0 0.1 miles
For more see
Top Experiences p62
Experiences p70
Eating p74
Drinking p76
Shopping p77
Pearl's Hill Reservoir
Pearl's Hill City Park
Park Cres
People's Park Complex
Chinatown
New Bridge Rd
Temple St
Smith St
Pearl's Hill Tce
Eu Tong Sen St
Outram Park
Outram Rd
Second Hospital Ave
Outram Park
Keong Saik Rd
Kreta Ayer Rd
Banda St
CHINATOWN
Tong Ah Eating House
Teck Lim Rd
Jiak Chuan Rd
Neil Rd
Duxton Hill
Bukit Pasoh Rd
Cantonment Rd
Duxton Rd
TANJONG PAGAR
Pinnacle@ Duxton
Craig Rd
Baba House
Everton Park
Everton Rd
Yan Kit Rd
Tanjong Pagar Plaza
Tanjong Pagar Rd
16
7
26
20
13
17
39
24
44
5
30
36
40
14
34
35
32
41
23
3

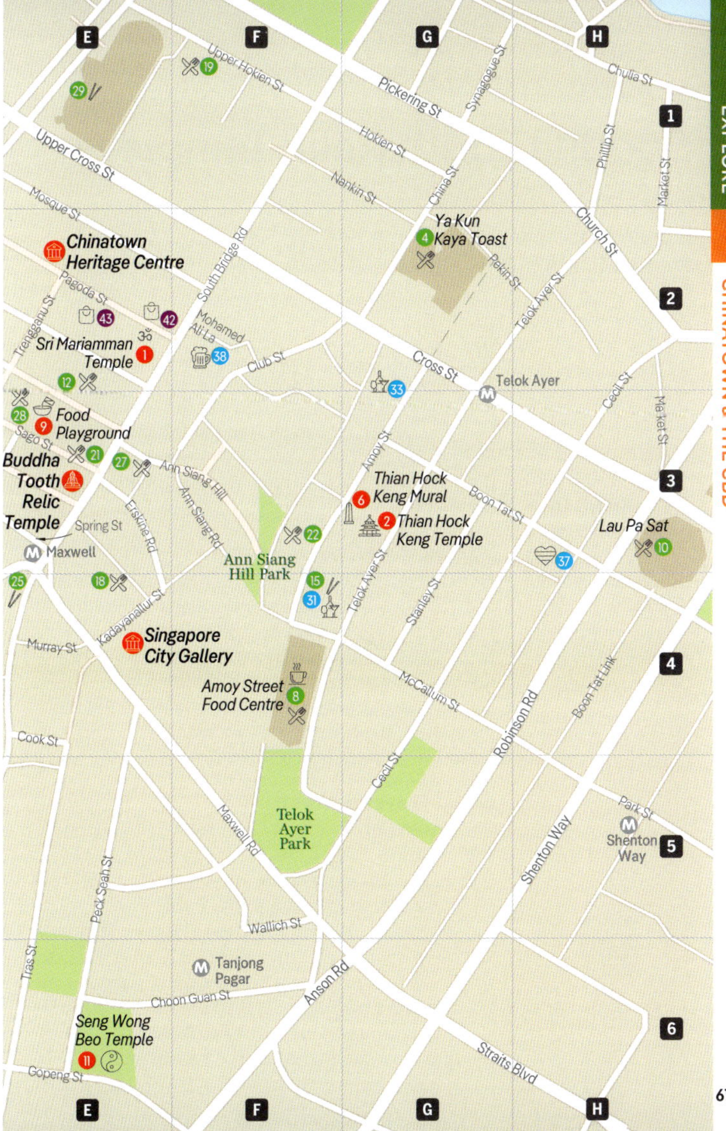
E
F
G
H
Upper Hokien St
Pickering St
Synagogue St
Chulia St
Upper Cross St
Hokien St
Phillip St
Market St
Mosque St
Nankin St
China St
Church St
Ya Kun Kaya Toast
Chinatown Heritage Centre
Pekin St
South Bridge Rd
Telok Ayer St
Pagoda St
Mohamed Ali La
Trengganu St
Sri Mariamman Temple
Club St
Cross St
Telok Ayer
Cecil St
Food Playground
Market St
Sago St
Amoy St
Buddha Tooth Relic Temple
Ann Siang Hill
Thian Hock Keng Mural
Boon Tat St
Ann Siang Rd
Erskine Rd
Spring St
Thian Hock Keng Temple
Lau Pa Sat
Maxwell
Ann Siang Hill Park
Telok Ayer St
Stanley St
Kadayanallur St
Singapore City Gallery
Murray St
Amoy Street Food Centre
McCallum St
Boon Tat Link
Robinson Rd
Cook St
Cecil St
Park St
Telok Ayer Park
Maxwell Rd
Shenton Way
Shenton Way
Peck Seah St
Wallich St
Tras St
Tanjong Pagar
Anson Rd
Choon Guan St
Seng Wong Beo Temple
Straits Blvd
Gopeng St
E
F
G
H
1
2
3
4
5
6

★ TOP EXPERIENCE

Buddha Tooth Relic Temple

Built in 2007, this hulking, Tang-style Chinese Buddhist temple is home to what is reputedly the left canine tooth of the Buddha. While its authenticity is debated, the compound remains an impressive display.

MAP P60 **E3**

PLANNING TIP
Open every day from 7am to 5pm (free). Respectful attire is a must. Cover-ups can be borrowed for free if needed.

VIP Status

The relic can be found on the 4th floor, inside a 320kg solid-gold stupa. Flanking the room are elevated platforms where you may sit or meditate, or head up the outside stairs to the peaceful rooftop garden where you can spin the world's largest cloisonné prayer wheel inside a 10,000 Buddhas Pagoda.

Storied Galleries

Housing artefacts collected from around the world, the 3rd-floor Buddhism museum charts Buddha's journey to enlightenment. The final chamber features crystalline *sariras* (relics) in golden reliquaries, believed to be collected after his cremation. A more eclectic mix of artwork is kept on the 2nd floor while the mezzanine has a startling set of wax figures depicting eminent monks around the world.

Grand Prayer Halls

The ground floor, with its two halls, is the liveliest. Facing South Bridge Rd, the Universal Wisdom Hall has worshippers depositing assorted offerings purchased from kiosks nearby. Two doorways at the sides lead into the Hundred Dragons Hall with a show-stopping Maitreya Buddha. Carved from a single log and painted with natural pigments, the commanding presence adds to the grandeur. For some vegetarian food, visit **Lian Xin** (p75), the temple's own food court in the basement.

Scan this QR code for a directory of the temple.

★ TOP EXPERIENCE

Chinatown Heritage Centre

Explore the gritty backstory of how Chinatown came to be at the immersive Chinatown Heritage Centre. Reopened in 2025 after an extensive refurbishment, visitors can expect an evocative experience across three multistorey shophouses.

Explore the Living Quarters

Begin with recreations of shophouse living in stunning detail, illustrating the stories of fictional characters, such as a clog maker or family of 10, through their accommodation. Personal objects and tools for their trade are placed around the cramped quarters as if they had just left their rooms, while scripted recordings played through scattered speakers mimic them calling out to one another in the unit.

Immigrant Hardships

Heading up to the 3rd floor, visitors get a glimpse of the challenges early migrants faced upon their arrival. The exhibition sheds light on both the historical chapters as well as the full social spectrum of Singapore's early Chinese settlers. From the perilous voyages to the local clans, it includes shadier aspects like opium dens and brothels that once defined the area, digging well beneath modern Chinatown's touristy veneer.

Customs & Heritage Finds

Finish with a gallery on local customs and festivals and perhaps even give the traditional toys a go. The immersive setups make this a perfect photo zone before you move on to an introduction of the existing local heritage businesses and hawkers – handy for exploring later.

MAP P60 **E2**

PLANNING TIP
Visit the centre (S$20) for context before you explore the area. The last portion includes bonafide local recommendations.

Scan this QR code to view the different tours and book tickets.

★ TOP EXPERIENCE

Baba House

Beautiful blue Baba House, one of Singapore's best-preserved Peranakan heritage homes, is a must-visit for those seeking to delve into its history and traditions. The National University of Singapore restored it to how it would have looked in the 1920s.

MAP P60 **A5**

PLANNING TIP
The one-hour small group tours are held Tuesday to Friday at 10am. All visits are by appointment only.

An Eye-Catching Entrance

This 1890s three-storey prewar **terrace house** *(babahouse.nus.edu.sg)* along Neil Rd was the ancestral home of the Wee family. The cobalt-blue facade is one of the few remaining frontages to be adorned with a high degree of Chinese-style plaster and brightly coloured porcelain ornamentation, featuring auspicious symbols like the phoenix for virtue, the crane for longevity and peonies for prosperity. Artisans created these using *jian nian* (cut and paste) technique, where broken ceramic pieces are joined to form 3D objects.

Peranakan Perfection

Step inside and marvel at the period furniture and antiques, as well as the building's elaborate architectural details. You'll learn the stories of the house and its former occupants, whose original family photos still grace the walls. The ornate bedrooms on the 2nd floor are a sight to behold: the *tenong* (wedding-gift box) takes pride of place.

A New Restoration

The 3rd-floor gallery has information on the research and materials used in the house's restoration, artefacts uncovered during on-site excavations and temporary exhibitions on Peranakan themes. The site is undergoing conservation, evaluation and repair and is scheduled to reopen in 2027.

Scan this QR code to book your visit.

★ TOP EXPERIENCE

Singapore City Gallery

Singapore didn't just happen; every inch was painstakingly planned. Dive into the free Singapore City Gallery for an insight into the city-state's urban landscape – witness its rapid evolution and innovative planning strategies, and glimpse its future.

Singapore: Vibrant City

Immerse yourself in a dramatic 270-degree panoramic film on a 12m screen, offering a 24-hour perspective on life in Singapore. Witness how Singaporeans work, live, eat and play, gaining an insight into the essence of 'home' for this island nation.

Galleries

Five galleries house the permanent collection, filled with numerous interactive exhibits. Delve into the narrative of Singapore's resolute land-reclamation policies, high-rise housing, meticulous urban planning and conservation efforts. You'll end the visit with a better appreciation of the tiny nation's challenges as it navigates a maturing populace, balancing important social, climate and conservation initiatives with visionary masterplans for its gleaming future.

Models

The **Central Area Model** and the **Island-Wide Model** offer bird's-eye views of Singapore. The former, a giant 3D model of the central district, is continuously updated to reflect Singapore's constantly changing urban landscape. Try to pinpoint where you are. The latter provides a macro-perspective, with a 1:1000 representation of the island. The accompanying three-minute projection shows the different planning strategies and key landmarks.

MAP P60 **E4**

PLANNING TIP

Aim to spend between one and two hours at the gallery *(ura.gov.sg/corporate/singapore-city-gallery; free)*. Weekday mornings are the quietest time to visit.

Scan this QR code for a self-guided tour with the Questeon app.

Walk Chinatown

While Singapore's Chinatown may be a tamer version of its former self, the area remains a visceral jungle of heady temples, medicinal curiosities, heritage shophouses and beloved hawker legends. So spend a few hours immersing yourself in this dynamic neighbourhood's sights, scents and flavours.

START	END	LENGTH
Nagore Durgha Shrine	People's Park Complex	1.3km; 1½hr

1 Chinatown's Immigrants

Near Telok Ayer MRT station, at the corner of Telok Ayer and Boon Tat Sts, you'll find the **Nagore Durgha Shrine**, a mosque built between 1828 and 1830 by Chulia Muslims from South India. It's now a free heritage centre and the three minarets symbolise the masts of ships for the shrine's patron saint of seafarers.

2 A Historic Hokkien Temple

Further on is the beautifully restored **Thian Hock Keng Temple** (p70), Chinatown's oldest and most revered Hokkien temple with spectacular carvings that can be seen from the facade alone. Outside, along the rear wall on Amoy St, awaits a 44m **mural** (p71) recounting the story of Singapore's early Hokkien immigrants.

3 Pause to Make a Wish

Continue on – passing the Al-Abrar Mosque, built in the 1850s – and turn right onto Amoy St, where at No 66 you'll see the tiny **Siang Cho Keong Temple**. Left of the entrance is a small 'dragon well' into which you can drop a coin and make a wish.

4 Heritage Shophouses

Adjacent to the temple stands an archway labelled Ann Siang Hill Rd. Pass through and ascend the walkway to Chinatown's apex, entering **Ann Siang Road**. Meander down this charming thoroughfare, adorned with exquisite shophouses that once housed Chinese guilds and clubs.

5 A Behemoth Buddhist Temple

At the end of the street, turn left onto South Bridge Rd and drop into the epic **Buddha Tooth Relic Temple** (p62). Further up South Bridge Rd you can see the triangular building of Jinriksha station, once the depot for hand-pulled rickshaws – now a Michelin-starred restaurant, Born.

6 Massive Chinatown Market

Upon exiting the temple, proceed along Sago St to the bustling **Chinatown Complex** (p75). Explore the vast hawker centre on the 2nd floor, offering an array of culinary delights, or venture to the basement to experience the lively wet market.

7 A Relaxing Finish

After leaving the Chinatown Complex, stroll along kitschy Trengganu St, turning left onto Pagoda St. Follow this path and cross the pedestrian bridge to arrive at **People's Park Complex** (p72), where you can indulge in a rejuvenating foot reflexology session.

Walk Tiong Bahru

Spend a late morning in Tiong Bahru, three stops from Raffles Pl on the East–West (green) MRT line. More than just hip boutiques, bars and cafes, this low-rise neighbourhood was Singapore's first public-housing estate and its art deco apartments now make for a retro architectural stroll.

START	END	LENGTH
Tiong Bahru Market	Bird Singing Corner	1.4km; 2hr

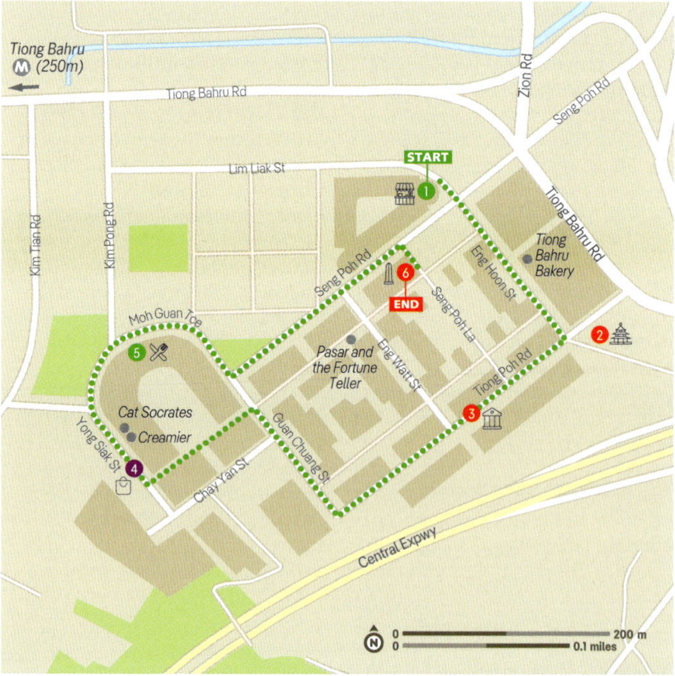

1 Buzzy Neighbourhood Market

Head into the **Tiong Bahru Market & Food Centre**, which remains staunchly old-school after a number of refreshes. The ground-floor wet market pumps at a frenetic pace, but one floor up you'll find the spacious and breezy hawker centre. Go for a wander to scoop out the eats on offer, and if you're feeling peckish, order takeaway.

2 Temple Tales

Exit the market and walk along Eng Hoon St – stopping for a caffeine hit at **Tiong Bahru Bakery** if needed – until you hit the intersection with Tiong Poh Rd. Opposite, you'll find smoky Qi Tian Gong Temple, dedicated to the monkey god. See how many you can count!

3 Awesome Architecture

From here, stroll southwest along **Tiong Poh Road**, before winding your way towards Yong Siak St. Take in the area's 1920s industrial-inspired architecture – the buildings here were constructed to resemble automobiles, trains, ocean liners and aeroplanes from that era.

4 Local Delights

Once you reach **Yong Siak Street**, spend some time ducking in and out of homegrown brand stores, sampling inventive flavours such as Sea Salt Gula Melaka from ice-cream parlour **Creamier** or picking up cutesy designer souvenirs at the quirky **Cat Socrates** (mind the feline shopkeepers).

5 Split Personality

Follow the road north as it curves, looking out for old-school corner noodle shop **Hua Bee**. If it's lunchtime, it will be doing a roaring trade, but after 3pm, the chefs of Dirty Supper take over, offering expertly grilled meats and whole-animal cooking to a different set of hungry throngs.

6 Mural Memories

Head northeast on Seng Poh Rd back towards the Tiong Bahru Market & Food Centre, and take a detour right down Seng Poh La to view the **Bird Singing Corner** mural, reminiscent of days long gone when residents would bring their songbirds here to hear them sing. The next alley to the right features the equally charming **Pasar and the Fortune Teller mural**.

EXPERIENCES

Be Enchanted by Sri Mariamman Temple

TEMPLE

MAP: 1 P60 **E2**

Paradoxically in the middle of Chinatown, **Sri Mariamman Temple** *(smt.org.sg)* stands as the oldest Hindu temple in Singapore, built in 1823 and rebuilt in 1843. You can't miss the Technicolor 1930s *gopuram* (tower) at the entrance, a defining feature of the South Indian Dravidian architectural style. Spend a few minutes walking the temple's perimeter, where you'll spot sacred-cow sculptures gracing the walls; the *gopuram* is embellished with plasterwork depictions of Brahma, Vishnu and Shiva, representing the trinity of creator, preserver and destroyer. That said, the complex is actually dedicated to the goddess Mariamman, known for her power in curing epidemic illnesses and diseases. Leave your shoes at the door and step inside to explore more ornate sculptures and murals, with each more colourful than the next.

Every October, the temple hosts the eye-opening **Thimithi festival**, during which Hindu devotees queue along South Bridge Rd and showcase their faith by hot-footing it over glowing coals.

Admire Symbolism at Thian Hock Keng Temple

TEMPLE

MAP: 2 P60 **G3**

Chinatown's oldest and most important Hokkien **temple** *(thianhockkeng.com.sg)* is often a haven of tranquillity. Built between 1839 and 1842 without nails or screws, it's a beautiful place dedicated to Mazu, the goddess of the sea. It was the favourite landing point of Chinese sailors before land reclamation pushed the sea far down the road. The temple's design features are richly symbolic: the stone lions at the entrance ward off evil spirits, while the painted depictions of phoenixes and peonies in the central hall symbolise peace and good tidings, respectively. During restoration works in 1998, one of the roof beams revealed a scroll written by the Qing emperor Guangxu, bestowing blessings on Singapore's Chinese community. The actual scroll is now on display at the National Museum of Singapore.

Hunt for unexpected figurines holding up the beams of the roof (ask for the free brochures at the front counter or scan the five QR codes found about the grounds).

Take in a Spectacular View at Pinnacle@Duxton

VIEWPOINT

MAP: 3 P60 **C5**

For killer city views at a bargain price, head to the 50th-floor rooftop of **Pinnacle@Duxton** *(pinnacleduxton.com.sg; S$6)*, the world's tallest public-housing complex. The project consists of seven 50-storey apartment towers connected by two levels of Skybridge which provide a 360-degree sweep of the city, port and sea. Find the discreet manned ticket booth at level one, Block G in the south, or use the digital kiosk which accepts credit cards and issues QR code tickets. Take lifts A or B up to the 50th floor and scan the ticket at the gate to pass (it may be fiddly). Chilling out is encouraged, with patches of lawn, modular furniture and sun loungers. Only 150 visitors are allowed each day. Sunset is the best time to visit.

Dip into the Breakfast of a Nation LOCAL EATS

If you want to immerse yourself in the Lion City, start your day with a Singaporean breakfast set. Not quite the standard version of eggs and toast many would know, this 'breakfast set' is made up of two barely boiled eggs (yolks runny and whites teetering on translucent), grilled slices of bread filled with pats of salty butter, and a generous spread of sweet, custardy *kaya* (coconut and egg jam) – all washed down with a cup of strong *kopi*. To eat, crack the eggs into the bowl, add a dash of soya sauce and white pepper, mix then dip in the *kaya* toast and enjoy. A solid place to experience this beloved Singapore staple is **Ya Kun Kaya Toast** (MAP: 4 P60 **G2**; *yakun.com*): the original shop location on China St is the best. For another take, Keong Saik Rd's old-timer **Tong Ah Eating House** (MAP: 5 P60 **C4**) serves thicker slices hand-toasted on charcoal.

Become Part of the Past STREET ART

MAP: 6 P60 **G3**

Amid Singapore's relentless progression from old to new, local self-taught artist Yip Yew Chong is keeping a touch of yesteryear alive with his incredibly detailed, 3D Singapore-heritage-scene artworks. You'll find the highest concentration in culturally rich Chinatown.

Begin your visual journey with his most impressive **mural** to date, a 44m masterpiece adorning the Thian Hock Keng Temple's rear wall that tells the story of the area's Hokkien immigrants. From here, it's a short walk to Mohamed Ali La, where another YC creation hawks his wares, and

PINK IN THE CITY

Chinatown includes a pocket of vibrant gay-owned businesses clustered along Neil Rd (p180). While Singapore is not exactly a leading destination for queer folks, there is no hostility from the public. In fact, partygoers often make it a point to have supper at the nearby Maxwell Food Centre, and the older hawker folks happily feed the pink brigade. Events-wise, for one weekend in June, Hong Lim Park transforms into a pink-soaked party with Pink Dot. The festival champions LGBTIQ+ rights, with performances and a pink light-up ceremony, but due to regulations, foreigners can only watch from outside the perimeters.

then onwards to Temple and Smith Sts, where numerous walls have been brought to life. Don't miss the colourful and dramatic *Cantonese Opera* at the junction of Temple St and South Bridge Rd.

Many of YC's murals incorporate interactive elements – an empty chair here, a bench spot there – inviting the viewer to become part of the heritage scene. Check Yip's website *(yipyc.com)* for locations.

Explore the People's Park Complex, a Neighbourhood Hub SHOPPING MALL

MAP: 7 P60 D1

Look up and you'll easily spot the red-and-white facade of the iconic **People's Park Complex** *(peoplesparkcomplex.sg)*: the building's striking brutalist design has loomed over the heart of Chinatown since the 1970s and was heralded as an architectural marvel of its time. Boasting an eclectic mix of market stalls, shops, eateries and residential apartments, the complex is a hive of activity inside, playing host to a dynamic blend of culture, commerce and community.

Wind your way through the market stalls on the ground floor to the cheap, no-frills reflexology booths (just what your tired feet ordered), the traditional Chinese medicine dispensaries, and the treasure trove of shops selling everything from textiles to electronics to Chinese antiques. To fuel up, the adjacent food centre is an unpretentious venue for legit hawker fare.

Photography lovers should head to the car park on level six (follow the signs), as the enormous yellow residential tower is one of Singapore's most clicked backdrops.

Taste the Future of Hawker Cuisine HAWKER

Hawker culture is deeply intertwined in Singapore's culinary DNA; a fact recognised when this dimension of the city's food scene earned a place on the UNESCO Intangible Cultural Heritage list in 2020.

But as the older generation of hawkers heads into retirement, many Singaporeans worry that this integral part of Singapore's national identity will be lost. Taking up the challenge, a new breed of hawkers is dishing out great meals on the cheap while infusing traditional recipes with unique twists. Chinatown's **Amoy Street Food Centre** (MAP: 8 P60 F4) is a hotbed of next-gen hawkers. Here you'll find A Noodle Story (p74; stall 01-39), serving bowls of perfected Singapore-style ramen; **Lagoon in a Bowl** (stall 01-48), where charred sous-vide salmon 'swims in a lagoon' of naturally dyed blue-butterfly-pea rice; and **Coffee Break** (stall 02-78), a humble drink stall putting some new spins on Singaporean *kopi* – black-sesame lattes and ginger-milk tea, anyone?

Cook Up the Classics at Food Playground

COOKING CLASS

MAP: 9 P60 **E3**

You've been gorging on Singapore's famous food, so why not learn to make it yourself? **Food Playground** *(foodplayground.com.sg; courses from S$120)* is a hands-on cooking school that explores Singapore's multicultural makeup through cuisine, as you prepare classic dishes such as laksa, nasi lemak (coconut rice) and *char kway teow* (stir-fried rice noodles with cockles, Chinese sausage and dark sauces). Courses usually run for three hours and kick off with an informative history of the dishes and an introduction to local ingredients. The best part, though, is undoubtedly when everyone tucks into their freshly cooked lunch. Classes book out early, so make sure to reserve your spot online.

A HAWKER GRAND DAME

Talk about ageing gracefully – propped up by frilly green cast-iron arches and crowned with a pavilion-shaped clock tower chiming every 15 minutes, **Lau Pa Sat** is still turning heads at 130 years old. First built as a coastal wet market in 1824, it moved locations several times before the elegant Victorian-style structure was completed in 1894. It has served as an iconic round-the-clock food destination ever since. Options are aplenty beneath its octagonal hall, but come after 7pm (3pm on weekends) when the outdoor streets become a paradise for satay (meat skewers).

MAP: 10 P60 **H3**

Learn about Marriages for the Departed at Seng Wong Beo Temple

TEMPLE

MAP: 11 P60 **E6**

Nestled discreetly behind metal gates next to Tanjong Pagar MRT station, little **Seng Wong Beo Temple** *(sengwongbeotemple.com)* is often overlooked by tourists. This Taoist temple is devoted to the Chinese City God, whose divine role encompasses safeguarding the city's prosperity and guiding departed souls to the underworld. However, Seng Wong Beo holds a unique distinction as the sole temple in Singapore that conducts ghost marriages. This ritualistic practice is intended to aid parents in arranging marriages for their departed children in the afterlife. A visit to the temple unveils intriguing customs and beliefs deeply rooted in Chinese folklore and spiritual traditions.

LISTINGS

Best Places for...

$ Budget $$ Midrange $$$ Top End

See p60 for map of locations

Eating

Moreish Noodles

A Noodle Story $
see 8 F4
The object of desire is Singapore-style ramen – Japanese pork slices with crunchy shrimp dumplings and *wanton mee* (noodles). *10am-8pm Mon-Fri, to 4pm Sat & Sun*

Noodle Man $
12 E2
Savour these perfectly chewy noodles, expertly hand-pulled right before your eyes at the open-kitchen counter and cooked with a variety of flavourful soups and sauces. *noon-3pm & 6-9pm*

Tai Wah Pork Noodle $
see 19 F1
Springy smooth noodles with just the right amount of bite and tart, vinegary flavours, the *bak chor mee* at this hawker stall is truly worth the wait. *9am-8.30pm Tue-Sun*

Rice Many Ways

Hawker Chan $
see 17 D2
It won, and then lost, a Michelin star, but the soya-sauce chicken rice, braised until savoury and tender, is definitely worth queuing up for. *10.30am-3.30pm Mon-Sat*

Lian He Ben Ji Claypot Rice $
see 17 D2
Famous for smoky claypot rice. Order the mixed option and expect a 30-minute wait, as each pot is cooked from scratch over charcoal stoves. *3-9pm Tue, Wed & Fri-Sun*

Tiong Shian Porridge $
13 D2
Pull up a stool and tuck into delicious congee (rice-based porridge). Winners include porridge with preserved egg or pork, and for the brave – claypot frog-leg porridge. *8am-4am Tue-Thu & Sun, to 4.30am Fri & Sat*

Delectable Dumplings

Zhong Guo La Mian Xiao Long Bao $
see 17 D2
Don't let the snaking queue put you off – these dumplings are worth the wait. The *xiao long bao* (soup dumpling) are a standout along with the Szechuan spicy wantons. *11am-8.30pm Wed-Fri, from 11.30am Sat & Sun*

Jing Hua Xiao Chi $
14 D4
Touted as Singapore's original dumpling house, this casual restaurant has a reputation for its savoury *xiao long bao* and crispy pan-fried dumplings. *11.30am-3pm & 5.30-9.30pm Tue-Sun*

Dumpling Darlings $$
15 F4
Experience deliciously crafted dumplings at this fuss-free eatery on trendy Amoy St. Choose from unique fillings such as smoked duck, truffle potato and Sriracha Crema. *11am-3pm & 5.30-10.30pm Tue-Fri & Sun, 5.30-10.30pm Sat & Mon*

Red Star $$

 D1

Experience old-school dim sum with trolley-clutching aunties rolling by with their steaming buffet of pork buns, rice-noodle rolls and assorted dumplings. *8.30am-2.30pm*

Hawker Centres

Chinatown Complex $

 D2

The hardcore hawker experience: a labyrinth of more than 260 stalls that are flooded during breakfast and lunch hours. Most stalls are shuttered by 8pm. *7am-10pm; stall hours vary*

Maxwell Food Centre $

 E4

One of Chinatown's most accessible hawker centres, Maxwell is a solid spot to savour some of the city's street-food staples. *8am-2am; stall hours vary*

Hong Lim Food Centre $

 F1

This old-school food centre is a Singapore foodie favourite. Only a few stalls open at night, so go for an early lunch to avoid the rush. *7am-7pm; stall hours vary*

Vegetarian & Vegan

Lian Xin Vegetarian Restaurant $

see p62

In the basement of the Buddha Tooth Relic Temple, this under-the-radar vegetarian food court offers an array of affordable and nourishing meals. *7am-5pm*

Yi Xin Vegetarian $

 D2

Choose your rice, get a good covering of curry sauce and point at dishes you'd like to try – three to four should suffice. Arrive before 11.30am for a seat. *8.30am-9pm Mon-Sat*

Eight Treasures Vegetarian Restaurant $$

 E3

Select from inventive Chinese dishes, with dietary needs clearly marked on the menu. Any questions are expertly answered by the staff. *11.30am-2.30pm & 6-9.30pm Tue-Fri, 11.30am-2.30pm & 5-9.30pm Sat & Sun*

Heritage Hawkers

Hill Street Fried Kway Teow $

see 17 D2

Slurp up silky rice noodles coated in a savoury-sweet sauce exploding with flavours of cockles, chinese sausage and pork lard. *9am-5pm Tue, Thu & Sat*

Millennium Glutinous Rice $

see 17 D2

Wake up early for this one. The addictive parcels of sweet or salty glutinous rice, aromatic with fried shallots and peanuts, sell out in hours. *7am Mon-Sat*

Chef Leung's Authentic Hand-Milled Rice Noodle Rolls $

see 17 D2

Quivering rice rolls swimming in a light sauce are the star here, prepared by a Raffles Hotel chef alumni. *6.30am-noon Thu-Sun*

Fine Dining

Cloudstreet $$$

 F3

Savour a 2½-hour culinary odyssey curated by Sri Lanka–born and Australia-trained chef-owner Rishi Naleendra, exploring diverse flavours and textures. *from 6.30pm Tue-Sat, from noon Fri & Sat*

Buko Nero $$

 D5

With just husband and wife on duty, this ultra-intimate affair is artful Italian featuring Asian-inspired twists from their market runs. *noon-3pm Thu-Sat, 6.30am-11.30pm Tue-Sat*

Olivia Restaurant & Lounge $$$

24 C3

Be transported to Barcelona with these tantalising dishes inspired by Catalan and Mediterranean cuisines. *6-10pm Mon, noon-2pm & 6-10.30pm Tue-Thu, noon-2.30pm & 6-10.30pm Fri-Sun*

Restaurant Born $$$

25 E4

Inhale eye-catching plates at the intersection of Chinese and French cuisine as you dine within a heritage rickshaw depot. *6-11pm Tue-Thu & Sat, noon-3pm & 6-11pm Fri*

Traditional Festive Treats

Lim Chee Guan $

26 D1

A Chinese New Year favourite, the pork jerky is grilled over charcoal to impart a delectable smokiness to the greasy slabs. *9am-10pm*

Tong Heng $

27 E3

Four generations on, the kitchen still rolls and moulds their Cantonese pastries by hand. The creamy diamond-shaped egg tarts are popular for celebrations. *9am-7pm*

Tai Chong Kok $$

 28 E3

Lotus-paste mooncakes are a must when mid-autumn comes around and these confectioners still make them from scratch by hand. *9am-8pm*

Thye Moh Chan $

 29 E1

The assortment of flaky Teochew biscuits make for quintessential gifts during weddings and births. *10am-9pm Sun-Thu to 9.30pm Fri & Sat*

Drinking

Curated Cocktails

No Sleep Club

 30 C4

A pop-up that is now an established star on Singapore's bar scene – unsurprising when its two owners are Singaporean cocktail legends. *4pm-midnight Tue-Sat, noon-6pm Sun*

Native

 31 F4

Surprising regional ingredients and clever twists result in memorable tipples at this drinking den on the upper floor of an Amoy St shophouse. *6pm-midnight Mon-Thu, to 1pm Fri & Sat*

Live Twice

 32 C4

This modest bar teleports you to 'cinematic' mid-century modern Japan with plush seating and sharp delicious libations. *6pm-midnight*

Employees Only

 33 G2

Look out for the 'psychic' sign and push past into this local outpost of the famous New York City cocktail bar for innovative cocktails. *5pm-1am Sun-Thu, to 2am Fri & Sat*

LGBTIQ+ Nightlife

Restroom Bar

 34 D4

The public-toilet facade is a hoot of a disguise for this speakeasy bar, which hosts go-go boys, DJ nights and drag shows. *8pm-1am Tue-Fri & Sun, to 2am Sat*

Carnival Haus

 35 D4

The cafe-by-day straps on its pink stilettos at night to invite an international crowd ready to sip on cocktails and mingle. *7pm-midnight*

Slippery Slope

 36 C4

Duck into a chic crimson hideaway with a more relaxed designer vibe serving pizzas with drinks, until the circuit-style music comes on at 10pm. *6pm-midnight.*

Sweat Club

 37 H3

On weekends this gay-friendly club welcomes the rainbow crew in the CBD, with three halls separately playing K-pop, EDM and DJ-led sets. *10pm-3am Fri, to 4am Sat*

Tap & Bottled Brews

Lion Brewery Co

 38 F2

The historic London craft brewery, reborn in Southeast Asia, seeks to redefine beer excellence. Its flagship taproom offers 25 beer taps for every flavour palate. *3-11pm Mon & Tue, from noon Sun, Wed & Thu, noon-1am Fri & Sat*

Smith Street Taps

see 17 D2

Head to this hawker-centre stall for a top selection of ever-changing craft and premium draught beers from around the world. Bring cash. *6-10.30pm Mon-Thu, to 11pm Fri, 2-11pm Sat*

Caffeine Hits

Lim's Café

see 17 D2

Combining Singaporean tradition with contemporary brewing techniques, this hawker stall crafts traditional *kopi* using an espresso machine. *9am-7pm Mon, to 6.30pm Tue, Sat & Sun, 8.30am-8.30pm Thu & Fri*

Glass Roasters

 39 A2

Find this slice of coffee heaven in the back lanes of Tiong Bahru. Explore the rotating bean selection or delight in the flavoured lattes. *7.30am-4.30pm Mon-Fri, 8.30am-6pm Sat & Sun*

Time for Tea

Tea Chapter

 40 D4

A serene teahouse where you can dive deep into the intricate art of Chinese tea ceremonies. Let the staff guide you on the ritual if you're new. *11am-9pm Sun-Thu, to 10.30pm Fri & Sat*

Shopping

Vintage Finds

Tong Mern Sern Antiques

41 D5

An Aladdin's cave packed to the gills with dusty furniture, books, woodcarvings, porcelain, and other bits and bobs; it's a hunting ground for Singapore nostalgia and treasure. *9.30am-5.30pm*

Née Vintage Store

42 E2

A welcoming boutique specialising in pre-loved vintage luxury items (with 100% authenticity guarantee), including handbags, jewellery, shoes and homewares from all the big-name fashion houses. *noon-7pm Tue-Sun*

Local Brands

Peranakan Tiles Gallery

43 E2

Owned by tile aficionado Victor Lim, this tile gallery and shop dazzles with bright hues. Feast your eyes on over 30,000 antique tiles, with select pieces available for purchase. *noon-6pm*

Ette Tea Company

44 D3

Dedicated to crafting contemporary tea blends infused with unique Singaporean and Southeast Asian flavours, including unexpected delights like Chicken Rice, Nasi Lemak and Pineapple Tart. *2.30-8pm Tue-Fri, 1-5.30pm Sat*

See p96 for eating, drinking and shopping listings

Explore Little India & Kampong Glam

Researched by Morgan Awyong

Little India, originally a settlement for Indian immigrants, is a bustling commercial and cultural hub. Serangoon Rd – the main thoroughfare – hosts businesses, restaurants and religious landmarks. The southern portion is particularly lively, a sensory feast. Affordable, authentic Indian cuisine is the star attraction.

A short walk southwest on Ophir Rd or a quick MRT ride to Bugis station leads to Kampong Glam. It's an intriguing snapshot of the intergenerational Islamic community: storybook mosques, third-wave cafes and eclectic boutiques dotted around brightly painted lanes. Haji Lane, the epicentre, comes alive in the late afternoon with live music and bar patrons spilling onto the pavements.

Getting Around

MRT

The two neighbourhoods are well connected by the MRT. Take the Downtown Line to Little India station to start your exploration, and choose Bugis for all things Kampong Glam.

Walking

The small streets, composed mostly of sheltered shophouses, are easy to explore on foot. Visit in the mornings or late afternoon for the most shade.

Bicycle

Cycling allows you to cover more ground but stay vigilant as the roads can be chaotic. Dense traffic and erratic pedestrians are the main challenges.

Sri Veeramakaliamman Temple (p88)

ZAC TAN/LONELY PLANET

THE BEST

MUSEUM Indian Heritage Centre (p82)

TEMPLE Sri Veeramakaliamman Temple (p88)

MOSQUE Sultan Mosque (p92)

COCKTAIL BAR Atlas (p99)

HAWKER CENTRE Tekka Centre (p83)

Haji Lane
Arab Street
Gelam Gallery
Kampong Glam
Farrer Park
Sri Srinivasa Perumal Temple
Petain Road Terraces
Mustafa Centre
Ayush Ayurvedic
Madame Mogra, Jasmine of the City
A Ride Through Race Course Road
Sri Veeramakaliamman Temple
LITTLE INDIA
Former House of Tan Teng Niah
Jln Besar Stadium
North Bridge Rd
Muscat St
Kandahar St
Baghdad St
Bussorah St
Bali La
Ophir Rd
Arab St
Haji La
Beach Rd
Owen Rd
Race Course Rd
Serangoon Rd
Petain Rd
Sturdee Rd
Beatty Rd
Foch Rd
Lavender St
Hamilton Rd
Cavan Rd
Jln Besar
Tyrwhitt Rd
Home Rd
Kitchener Rd
Verdun Rd
Kinta Rd
Chander Rd
Race Course La
Syed Alwi Rd
Sam Leong Rd
Plumer Rd
Desker Rd
Baboo La
Hindoo Rd
Kampong Kapor Rd
Rowell Rd
Norris Rd
Maude Rd
King George's Ave
Townshend Rd
Jln Berseh
Kelantan La
Veerasamy Rd
Belilios La
Kerbau Rd
Cuff Rd
French Rd
0 50 m
0 200 m
0 0.1 miles

Little India
Tekka Centre
Moghul Sweets
Thandapani Co
Indian Heritage Centre
Little India Arcade
Boy with a $100 Bill
Abdul Gafoor Mosque
Jalan Besar
Rochor
Kampong Glam Cemetery
Rochor Canal
Vintage Camera Museum
Sultan Mosque
Malay Heritage Centre
KAMPONG GLAM
See Kampong Glam Enlargement
Kwan Im Thong Hood Cho Temple
Bugis Street Market
Bugis
Parkview Square; Parkview Museum
For more see
Top Experiences p82
Experiences p88
Eating p96
Drinking p98
Shopping p99
Buffalo Rd
Upper Dickson Rd
Bukit Timah Rd
Clive St
Campbell La
Madras St
Dalhousie Ln
Hastings Rd
Dunlop St
Perak Rd
Dickson Rd
Upper Weld Rd
Jln Besar
Kelantan Rd
Weld Rd
Mayo St
Sungei Rd
Rochor Canal Rd
Albert St
Short St
Selegie Rd
Prinsep St
Bencoolen St
Waterloo St
Queen St
Rochor Rd
Victoria St
Ophir Rd
Arab St
Jln Kubor
Syed Alwi Rd
Syed Alwi Bridge
Jln Pinang
Jln Pisang
North Bridge Rd
Jln Sultan
Aliwal St
Kandahar St
Sultan Gate
Pahang St
Baghdad St
Bussorah St
Haji La
Beach Rd
A
B
C
D
E
F
5
6
7
8

★ TOP EXPERIENCE

Indian Heritage Centre

Housed in a stunning modern building, the well-curated Indian Heritage Centre showcases the diverse history and contributions of Singapore's Indian community, charting the vibrant narrative of the diaspora, from early settlers to contemporaries.

MAP P80 **B5**

PLANNING TIP
Free guided one-hour tours are offered from Tuesday to Sunday at 11am, with additional 2pm time slots on Friday, Saturday and Sunday.

Scan this QR code for opening hours and booking information.

A Walk Through History

The **museum** *(indianheritage.gov.sg; adult/student/child under 6 S$10/8/free)* is divided into five captivating themes from the 1st century CE to today, each offering a unique perspective on Indian culture and its profound influence in Singapore. As you explore the extensive collection of historical artefacts, archival footage and multimedia displays, you will delve into the early interactions between South Asia and Southeast Asia, and learn about Indian cultural traditions and the invaluable contributions of Indian Singaporeans to the nation's development. The centre also houses a rooftop garden and activity spaces.

The Architecture

Drawing inspiration from the *baoli* (Indian stepped well), the museum's main facade mirrors the pattern of the flights of steps in the well that lead down to the water table. You'll be able to experience this as part of the museum route when descending from the top floor. As the sun sets, the building's translucent facade undergoes a magical transformation, revealing the mural that lies behind it like a kaleidoscopic tapestry.

Chettinad Doorway

One of the museum's standout attractions is a remarkable 19th-century Chettinad doorway, richly detailed with an astonishing 5000 carvings – a glimpse of the exquisite craftsmanship of the past.

★ TOP EXPERIENCE

Tekka Centre

Located next to Little India MRT station, the Tekka Centre is often hailed as the beating heart of Little India – and boy, does it get pumping! Encompassing a wet market, a food centre and a range of shops, it's loud, busy and a riot of colour.

MAP P80 **A5**

Buzzing Market

Singapore's most extensive wet market is laden with tropical fruits, Asian vegetables, aromatic herbs and a galaxy of spices. Keep an eye out for **Lim's Coconuts & Sundry Products**, where you can watch a mesmerising old-school grating machine churn out fluffy white coconut pulp. There's also a wide selection of meats and seafood, often presented in their 'original condition', so expect to witness lots of cutting, chopping and slicing. If that isn't your cup of tea, navigate this area with caution.

PLANNING TIP
If you don't like crowds, steer clear of Little India on Sunday. It is the only day off for many of the city's construction workers, who converge, run errands and trade.

Tasty Eats

Once you've feasted your eyes and maybe made a few purchases, head to the hawker area to fill up on some delicious Indian fare. Join the queue for real-deal biryani, paper-thin *dosa* (lentil-flour pancakes), fluffy *roti prata* (dough-flour pancakes) and delectable *murtabak* (stuffed savoury pancakes). Wash it all down with some creamy *teh tarik* (pulled tea).

A Sea of Colour

Venture up one floor and you'll encounter a rainbow-coloured sea of Indian sari and textile stores, as well as a small battalion of skilled tailors. This is probably the most budget-friendly place to pick up an Indian outfit. While prices are marked, some well-mannered bargaining is worth a try.

Scan this QR code to book a tour of the Tekka Market with SingaBites.

WALKING TOUR

Walk Little India

Loud, colourful and refreshingly raffish, Little India stands in contrast to the more sanitised parts of the city. Dive into a wonderland of spice stores, gold and sari traders, and rainbow-coloured temples. Jumble them up with a booty of fiery eateries, and you have Singapore's most hypnotic urban experience.

START	END	LENGTH
Sri Srinivasa Perumal Temple	Tekka Centre	1.7km; 1½hr

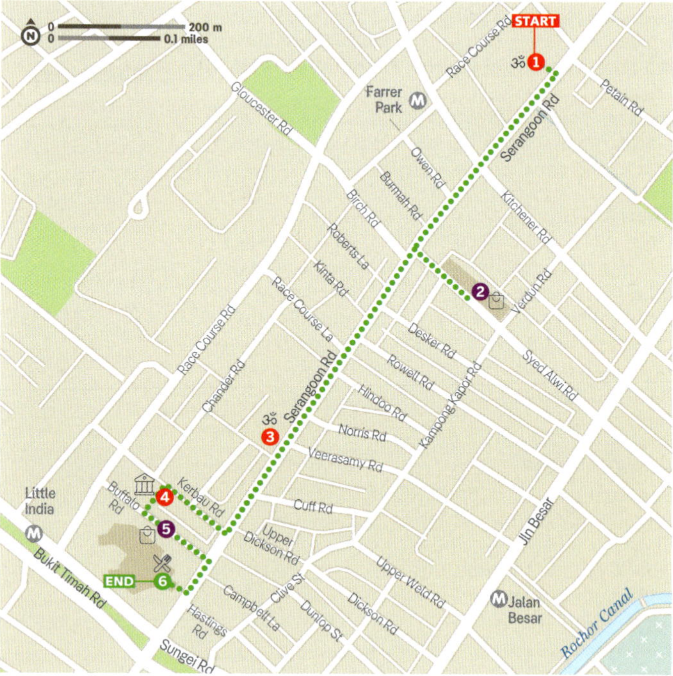

1 A Technicolour Tower

Just northeast of the Farrer Park MRT, along Serangoon Rd, spot the striking 20m-tall *gopuram* (tower) of the **Sri Srinivasa Perumal Temple** (p89) with its ornate and colourful carvings that cost S$300,000 to build. The temple dates back to 1855 and is Singapore's first temple for worshippers of Lord Vishnu, created in the traditional South Indian–style architecture.

2 Shop Till You Drop

Returning to Serangoon Rd, proceed southwest and turn left onto Syed Alwi Rd, where blessings transition into bargains at the colossal **Mustafa Centre** (p88). Crammed ceiling high with goods, with many directly from India, a spot of retail therapy here can end up with you getting lost in a sea of groceries, household products and electronics.

3 Be Moved by Prayer

Further on Serangoon Rd is the **Sri Veeramakaliamman Temple** (p88), Little India's main Hindu temple. It's dedicated to the ferocious goddess Kali who is very popular in Bengal, the birthplace of the labourers who built the structure in 1881. The temple is at its most evocative during each of the four daily *puja* (prayer) sessions.

4 A Kaleidoscope of Colour

Exit the temple and continue along Serangoon Rd, turning right when you reach Kerbau Rd. Wander along and be dazzled by the **Former House of Tan Teng Niah** (p90), a two-storey Chinese bungalow that's quite possibly Singapore's most colourful building and, architecturally, the last of its kind. The candy-coloured structure is a photogenic backdrop.

5 Follow Your Nose

Once you're Instagrammed out, take the side alley to **Buffalo Road**. It's a bustling strip packed with Indian produce shops, Hindu shrines and sweetly perfumed garland stalls. Flowers used to make the garlands are highly symbolic: both the lotus and the white jasmine spell purity, while the yellow marigold denotes joy and abundance.

6 Little India's Beating Heart

Finally, slip into the **Tekka Centre** (p83) opposite for some wet-market exploration and plenty of cheap and tasty food. A *teh tarik* here is a satisfying reward at the end of the walk. If you're after a sari, the top floor has a swarm of vendors ready to advise and deal.

WALKING TOUR

Walk Kampong Glam

Try not to get whiplash as you wander about Kampong Glam, once the residence of the local sultan. Between its gleaming mosque icon, spontaneous street art and aesthetic cafes in rustic pre-war shophouses, the neighbourhood is a buzzing riot of contrasts that will have your head swivelling.

START	END	LENGTH
Malay Heritage Centre	Haji Lane	1.1km; 1hr

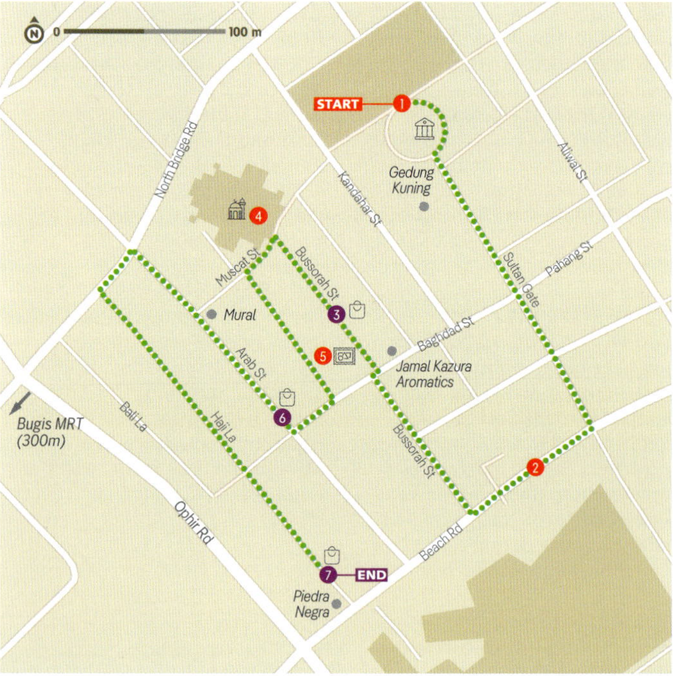

1 The Seat of Royalty

Exiting Bugis MRT, head northwest along North Bridge Rd before turning right onto Kandahar St. On your left will be the **Malay Heritage Centre** (p92), formerly the istana (palace) for Singapore's last sultan. Having explored Malay-Singaporean culture and history, head southeast to the main gate.

2 A Former Beach

Continue down Sultan Gate, passing by Gedung Kuning ('yellow mansion' in Malay) on your right. Once a residence for Malay royalty, it's now a restaurant and event space. Upon reaching **Beach Road** – which is no longer on the beach, thanks to land reclamation – turn right and peek at the trendy boutiques and eateries.

3 Snap a Picture-Perfect Street

Turn right at **Bussorah Street** and stroll between the beautifully restored shophouses on either side. Most began as shops selling pilgrimage wares for Muslims heading to Mecca, and some, such as **Jamal Kazura Aromatics** (p99), remain. The street's tall palm trees elegantly frame the mosque, creating a picture-perfect *Arabian Nights* scene.

4 Visit a Fairytale Mosque

At the end of the lane is the historic **Sultan Mosque** (p92). Designed in the Saracenic style and topped by a golden dome, it's the largest mosque in Singapore. Visitors are welcome and non-Muslims can view the prayer hall through a grill fence. After exiting, head southwest down Muscat street.

5 Wander an Art-Filled Alley

After passing beneath a large granite arch with Omani carvings, you enter a backlane where **Gelam Gallery** (p92) is located. Here, an array of vibrant street art showcases the talents of students as well as local and international artists. Early mornings are best for visiting before the delivery trucks arrive.

6 Dive into Old-Time Trades

As you exit at Baghdad St, turn right into **Arab Street** (p93), the area's traditional textile district. Here you'll find all manner of fabrics, cane wares, Persian carpets, lanterns, and perfumes. Don't miss the **mural** at No 92 by Singaporean artist Yip Yew Chong, which vividly captures the neighbourhood's history and heritage.

7 The Trendiest Lane

Emerging at North Bridge Rd, take two lefts onto the narrow, candy-hued **Haji Lane** (p93). Explore quirky boutiques and admire the fun street art, or snap some themed booth photos. Finish by pulling up a stool at **Piedra Negra**, a Mexican and margarita powerhouse with the lane's most iconic mural.

EXPERIENCES

Be Awed by the Sri Veeramakaliamman Temple

TEMPLE

MAP: 1 P80 **B4**

Little India's colourful, visually striking **Sri Veeramakaliamman Temple** *(srivkt.org)* is dedicated to the ferocious goddess Kali. Adorned with a garland of skulls, she is depicted tearing apart her victims while also engaging in serene family moments with her sons Ganesh and Murugan! The bloodthirsty consort of Shiva has long been revered in Bengal, the birthplace of the labourers who constructed the building in 1881. Its most notable feature, the entrance *gopuram* (tower) with intricate carvings of Hindu deities, was added in the 1980s. The striped red walls pay homage to its earlier incarnation. Visitors are welcome inside the temple during designated hours and the temple is at its most evocative during the four daily *puja* (prayer) sessions. Leave your shoes at the door and be enveloped in the aroma of incense, the rhythmic melodies of temple music and the chants of prayers. Photography is allowed, but be mindful that this is an active site of worship.

Meander Through the Markets of Little India

SHOPPING AREA

Spend an hour or so exploring the **Little India Arcade** (MAP: 2 P80 **A5**; *littleindiaarcade.com.sg*), a modest but colourful area of wall-to-wall shops, pungent aromas and Hindi film music – a welcome contrast to the prim modernity of many parts of the city. It's the place to come to pick up that framed print of Krishna you've always wanted, eat great food and watch streetside cooks fry chapatis. For sweet treats, head to **Moghul Sweets** (MAP: 3 P80 **A5**) – the *gulab jamun* (syrup-soaked fried dough balls) and *barfi* (condensed milk and sugar slice) are highlights.

Inhale Heady Spices at Thandapani Co

SPICE SHOP

MAP: 4 P80 **B5**

Stroll down to Dunlop St, just behind the Indian Heritage Centre, and seek out the legendary spice store **Thandapani Co**, named after the founder's favourite deity. Not much has changed here since the shop opened in the 1960s: it still has hessian bags packed with chillies, fennel seeds and other Indian culinary staples. This is considered one of the best spice vendors in the city; you'll be rubbing shoulders with home cooks and professional chefs alike, all stocking up on ingredients that are hard to find elsewhere on the island.

Shop for Bargains at Mustafa Centre

SHOPPING MALL

MAP: 5 P80 **C3**

Long revered as Singapore's epicentre of bargain shopping, the labyrinthine **Mustafa Centre** *(mustafa.com.sg)* stocks it all.

From gold jewellery to electronics, fabrics to fashion, luggage to beauty products, its six levels are claustrophobically packed to the brim. Open around the clock every single day, it is one of those reliable places you can procure a wheelchair or gold chain at 3am. Within the commercial hub are also money-changers and a supermarket on the 2nd floor with a wide range of Indian and international foodstuffs. If you don't like crowds, skip the post-work peak hour and don't even think about visiting on Sundays. Otherwise, set aside a few hours and accept that you'll most likely get lost in the endless rows of products. Once you're done, head outside to **Mustafa Cafe** on Syed Alwi Rd for a warming cup of masala tea.

Be Dwarfed by the Sri Srinivasa Perumal Temple TEMPLE

MAP: 6 P80 **D1**

Dating from 1855, the **Sri Srinivasa Perumal Temple** *(sspt.org.sg)* is dedicated to Vishnu, the Hindu god who restores the balance between good and evil. In 1966, a 20m-tall *gopuram* (tower) was added, enhancing its grandeur. Step inside to encounter statues of Vishnu, Lakshmi and Andal, and Vishnu's bird-mount, Garuda, creating a divine sanctuary enriched with history and artistry. The temple holds great significance during the annual **Thaipusam festival** (usually held in February), as it is the starting point for a colourful, wince-inducing street parade. To show their unwavering faith and devotion, many participants pierce their bodies with hooks and skewers yet exhibit little signs of pain or bleeding. Despite the graphic nature, the event is one of celebration with live music and spirited community worship.

BEST HIDDEN STREET ART IN LITTLE INDIA

A Ride Through Race Course Road

MAP: 7 P80 **A4**

In an alley beside 50 Race Course Rd, an errant jockey has kicked up a vendor's wares – a nod to the former racetrack nearby.

Madame Mogra, Jasmine of the City

MAP: 8 P80 **A3**

Gawk at the glorious blooming jasmine at 27 Chander Rd. Walk deeper into the alley and find a migrant worker earnestly nurturing the plant.

Boy with a $100 Bill

MAP: 9 P80 **B6**

Blink and you'll miss this cheeky boy dangling a large bill to tempt passers-by beside Perak Hotel.

Admire the Whimsical Abdul Gafoor Mosque

MOSQUE

MAP: 10 P80 **B6**

A little bit of this and that: with its compelling mix of Saracenic, Moghul and European elements, the **Abdul Gafoor Mosque** *(facebook.com/masjidabdulgafoor)* turns heads with its commanding symmetry and exquisite details. Built in 1907 and restored several times over, the final result is an awe-inspiring masterpiece. Every facet of its Corinthian columns and balustrades are outlined in deep palm green, accompanied by beautiful cinquefoil arches and mini-minarets that add to its magical castle effect. Rising above the entrance and speckling of stars against the white walls is a sunburst pattern. It radiates, in elegant Arabic calligraphy, the names of 25 major Islamic prophets. Within, a central cupola dominates the prayer hall, made majestic with spiralling columns, coloured glass windows and a glittering chandelier. A Heritage Centre invites visitors to explore the mosque's rich history and gain insight into the Islamic faith.

Spot the Eye-Popping Former House of Tan Teng Niah

ARCHITECTURE

MAP: 11 P80 **A4**

Near Tekka Centre stands a rainbow-coloured two-storey Chinese bungalow, the **Former House of Tan Teng Niah** *(free)*. The house harks back to a bygone era when Chinese industries were a fixture of this neighbourhood. It's believed to be the sole surviving building of its kind in the area – the rest were demolished to make way for more modern developments. Tan Teng Niah operated numerous local businesses, including a rubber smoke house and several confectionary factories. Willy Wonka would have approved of this technicoloured tribute in the 1900 monument. The building was restored and conserved in the 1980s and designated for commercial use. While it's not possible to enter, its psychedelic facades are a

DITCH THE CUTLERY

Eating with your fingers is customary in India, and you'll see this regularly in Singapore's Indian restaurants. To try it yourself, start by washing your hands. If your meal comes with bread, tear off small pieces and fold small bites into them before popping the little parcel into your mouth. Be sure to only use your right hand for eating. Meals with rice are trickier – combine a little rice with your accompanying dish to form a small ball, then lift it to your mouth and push it in with your thumb. It may take some practice, but it's a messily enjoyable experience, and one likely greeted with appreciation from locals.

favourite subject for photographers and social media fodder.

Revive Yourself at Ayush Ayurvedic

MASSAGE

MAP: 12 P80 B3

If the frenetic pace of Little India has left you feeling frazzled, surrender yourself to the tranquil rejuvenation of Ayurveda, the Indian system of medicine based on ancient writings that rely on a natural and holistic approach to physical and mental health. Regarded as a health clinic, its treatments feel wonderfully spa-like. Experience Abhyangam, a soothing massage using medicated oils, or try Shirodhara, where warm oil is rhythmically poured onto your forehead (the third eye). A herbal steam bath, where you sit in a large wooden box up to your neck, is recommended to accompany most treatments to help detoxify the body. There are numerous centres scattered throughout the area; our pick is **Ayush Ayurvedic** *(ayurvedasg.com; 50min treatments from S$70)*. After a consult with a doctor, staff usher you into a treatment room. Benefits can be felt immediately but repeated visits will ensure the best results. Given how soothing they are, that won't be a problem.

Caffeinated Throwbacks at Jalan Besar

NEIGHBOURHOOD

Jalan Besar ('big/wide road' in Malay) was once known for boxing matches and hardware shops. Beginning as a betel-nut and fruit orchard, it saw milestone developments in the form of New World Park (1923), Grand Theatre (1958) and the Jalan Besar Stadium (1929), which used to be a key site for important matches. Only the latter remains. These days, it's a blend of charming heritage architecture and artisan cafes. Leading the renaissance around the 2010s, **Chye Seng Huat Hardware** (p98; *cshhcoffee.com*) kickstarted the third-wave coffee revolution by establishing a roastery and cafe here. Several trendy businesses followed, making Jalan Besar a buzzy area. While past its heyday, the handful of hip coffee joints and bakeries in this neighbourhood (mostly along Tyrwhitt Road) still offer a charming off-itinerary break.

View Peranakan Perfection on Petain Road

BUILDING

MAP: 13 P80 E2

While in the Jalan Besar neighbourhood, check out the exceptional row of lavishly adorned double-storey **Petain Road Terraces**. These Peranakan beauties, dating back to the 1920s, showcase an explosion of colour, from the floral-motif ceramic wall tiles to the pillar bas-reliefs adorned with flowers, birds and trees. The hyper-ornate decoration represents the distinctive characteristics of the late shophouse style.

Be Enchanted by the Fairytale Sultan Mosque

MOSQUE

MAP: 14 P80 **E7**

Singapore's grandest mosque, seemingly pulled from an *Arabian Nights* storybook, **Sultan Mosque** *(sultanmosque.sg)* is nothing short of enchanting. Founded in 1824 by Sultan Hussein Shah, it was one of his key requests to Raffles and the East India Company, made in conjuction with the signing of a land treaty and his continued sovereignty over the area. In 1932, the original single-storey brick mosque was replaced by the present building, designed by Irish architect Denis Santry. Gazetted as a national monument in 1975, it showcases Indo-Saracenic style and boasts two majestic golden domes and two eight-storey minarets that can be seen from afar. Visitors are welcome from 10am to noon and 2pm to 4pm every day except Friday. Non-Muslims should not enter the main prayer hall, but you can still appreciate its inner beauty through a wide-grilled gate. All visitors are expected to dress suitably (cloaks and skirts are available at the entrance).

Visit a Seat of Royalty at the Malay Heritage Centre

MUSEUM

MAP: 15 P80 **F7**

The area of Kampong Glam is the historic seat of Malay royalty, resident here before the arrival of Sir Stamford Raffles. The *istana* (palace) on this site was built for the last sultan of Singapore, Ali Iskandar Shah, between 1836 and 1843. Its buttery-yellow buildings were converted into the **Malay Heritage Centre** *(malayheritage.gov.sg)* in 2015, and its galleries explore Malay-Singaporean culture and history, chronicling the early migration of traders to Kampong Glam and the evolution of Malay-Singaporean cinema, theatre, music and publishing. It reopened in 2026 after a revamp, with outdoor galleries and interactive activities.

Ponder the Back-Alley Gelam Gallery

STREET ART

MAP: 16 P80 **B1**

It's not just the prominent streets that steal the limelight in Kampong Glam. The back alleys on either side of pedestrianised Bussorah St have come to life with **Gelam Gallery** *(free)*, Singapore's first permanent outdoor art space. Rear walls have been transformed into canvases and now boast artworks by more than 30 artists. Some are painstaking full-wall renderings while others are intricate entities that might be easily missed. This artistic ensemble features the work of newly graduated students from esteemed institutions such as Nanyang Academy of Fine Arts (NAFA) and LASALLE College of the Arts, as well as pieces by experienced local and international artists. Dustbins and the occasional chair or broom might litter the scene but it's all part of the organic charm. Come early if you want to take pictures to avoid the delivery vehicles that park here.

Shop in the Reinvented Muslim Quarter

SHOPPING DISTRICT

Begin your retail adventure on pedestrianised **Haji Lane** (MAP: 17 P80 **A1**), a narrow street lined with pastel-hued shophouses that host an eclectic mix of quirky boutiques, vintage shops, hole-in-the-wall craft-beer bars and plenty of high-impact street art. Although establishments seem to change rapidly – likely due to sky-high rents – you'll be relieved to find that, so far, generic chain stores haven't infiltrated the area. Instead, up-and-coming independent designers and charming cafes clamour for a foothold, ensuring there's always something new to check out.

One block over awaits **Arab Street** (MAP: 18 P80 **B1**), with stores that showcase more traditional wares including fabrics, carpets and scarves. Make sure to visit Dilip Textiles (p99), a one-stop shop for vibrant block-printed table linens at affordable prices. Another must-visit is Sifr Aromatics (p99), a perfume emporium specialising in custom blends – here you can immerse yourself in a treasure trove of olfactory delights.

SOUL SEARCHING

Kampong Glam's anti-mall crowd have nourished the eclectic offerings of the neighbourhood, giving rise to some unforeseen trends. Floating in with crystals, tarot and meditations, a holistic wave began with Going Om and Sanctum before 2010. Along the way, others like The Song of the Self, Life by Design and 3 of Cups took root, though all have since closed. The legacy remains in the form of casual roadside readings in the evenings on Haji Lane (weekends are best) and at Qi New Age Healing on Kandahar St, offering consultations, workshops and tools of the magical trade.

Feel Off-Kilter at Hajjah Fatimah Mosque

MOSQUE

MAP: 19 P80 **F7**

If you venture away from the city along Beach Rd, you'll come across **Hajjah Fatimah Mosque** *(masjidhajjahfatimah.sg)*, erected in 1846. This historic place of worship is one of the few in Singapore to be named after a female figure. It pays homage to Hajjah Fatimah, a Melaka-born philanthropist whose residence is believed to have stood on the site. Distinguished by its peculiar architecture, the mosque combines Middle Eastern and European styles; its most notable features include a bulbous dome and a Moorish wooden balcony alongside European-style pilasters and a minaret that resembles a church spire. The holes in the tower once held lanterns to light the way for sailors. The minaret's distinctive lean, approximately six degrees from the centre and visible from the front, has granted the mosque the moniker of Singapore's Leaning Tower.

Partake in an Art Deco Extravaganza at Parkview Square LANDMARK BUILDING

Resembling a structure plucked from the *Batman* series, the magnificent bronze tower of **Parkview Square** (MAP: 20 P80 **D8**; *parkviewsquare.com*), with its brooding gargoyles, is inspired by the Chanin Building in New York City. Its open-air plaza has an array of statues and sculptures – most notably a majestic golden crane poised to take flight. Stroll around the compound and see if you can spot luminaries like Shakespeare or Mozart.

On the 3rd floor is the **Parkview Museum** *(adult/child S$25/15)* managed by Groundseesaw. Focusing on immersive visual art, the projections have drawn from the captivating works of Klimpt, Van Gogh and Monet. The visual indulgence doesn't stop there. The jaw-dropping interior of Parkview Square's 15m-high lobby is adorned with marble floors, gilded brass and intricate frescoes. It sets the stage for the centrepiece – the upscale Atlas (p99) bar with a 12m-high gin wall. Be prepared to make reservations way in advance.

Say Cheese at the Vintage Camera Museum MUSEUM

MAP: 21 P80 **E6**

Calling all photography enthusiasts! Step into the lens – quite literally – at the **Vintage Camera Museum** *(vintagecamerasmuseumsg.com; S$20)*. Shaped like a camera, this unique museum showcases a diverse collection of classic cameras and photography equipment. From iconic brands to rare gems, explore pieces spanning various eras and technologies, including intriguing replicas like the Mammoth Camera and whimsical gadgets like an 11-gram camera. Dive into vintage lenses, film rolls and accessories, each narrating tales of innovation and creativity. Ever wondered what the first picture taken in Singapore was? You'll find it here. There's an admission fee and you must book online, but it's definitely worth it if you're a camera geek.

Pray for Luck at Kwan Im Thong Hood Cho Temple TEMPLE

MAP: 22 P80 **B8**

Amid the lively sounds of *chien tung* (Chinese fortune sticks) rattling in their tins lies one of Singapore's most bustling temples. Devoted to the popular goddess of mercy, Kuan Yin (Guan Yin), **Kwan Im Thong Hood Cho**

Temple *(facebook.com/kwanimthonghoodchotemple)* is a cherished destination for those seeking good fortune. On the eve of every Chinese New Year, devotees will race to be the first to plunge their sticks into the main incense urn to claim the freshest blessings of the year. The temple's colourful facade exemplifies the craftsmanship popular in the late 19th century, with grand pagoda rooftops and ornate carvings showcasing motifs including dragons, phoenixes and water lilies. The entrance buzzes with elderly vendors peddling flowers or fortunetelling.

Up the street, believers rub the belly of a majestic bronze Buddha Maitreya, hoping for an extra dose of luck. In a very Singaporean case of religious pragmatism, worshippers also offer prayers at the polychromatic Hindu **Sri Krishnan Temple** *(facebook.com/SriKrishnanTemple)* next door.

ALL IN THE NAME

North of Kampong Glam's majestic mosque, a series of small parallel lanes buzz with cafes and eateries, with the exception of one – **Jalan Kubor**. Street names in Singapore often point to their origins, and while the rest have associations with produce like bananas (pisang) and betel nut (kledek), kubor in Malay means 'grave'. Prior to commercial takeover, this grim lane was known for its funeral parlours. These are no longer around, but you can still visit Singapore's oldest Muslim cemetery just across Victoria St with prominent Muslim figures including royalty from the Johor Sultanate in Malabar Mosque nearby.

Bargain-Hunt at Bugis Street Market

SHOPPING MARKET

MAP: 23 P80 **C8**

Steel yourself: **Bugis Street Market** is that rare messy retail phenomenon in Singapore that is both rowdy and rollicking. Regardless of their wares, shops here vie for your eye with bright lights and blaring music, while food stalls have the olfactory advantage with their sugarcane, fried snacks and grilled pork jerkies. And yes – there are durians too at this perpetual *pasar malam* (night market). Even though the main route takes all of five minutes to complete, the sea of shoppers will slow your pace to a crawl. Either that, or you'll be swept away into the smaller maze-like corridors, lured by a bargain garment or kitschy mobile-phone accessory. If you're somewhat of a tomb raider, with some luck, you might find the escalators to the upper levels providing air-conditioned relief, and beauty services such as manicures and ear piercings. Our best advice here: come with no agenda and surrender to the chaos.

LISTINGS

Best Places for...

See p80 for map of locations

$ Budget $$ Midrange $$$ Top End

Eating

Heritage Treats

Sri Aachi Aappakadai $
24 A5
Indulge in freshly made *appams* (rice pancake), cooked to perfection with a spongy centre and crispy edges. Request a sprinkle of grated coconut, dust with red sugar and enjoy. *6am-9pm*

Ar Rahman Royal Prata $
25 A5
This Tekka Centre stall flips some of Singapore's finest *murtabak* (stuffed savoury pancake). Our pick is the mutton; wash it down with a lassi from the stall next door. *7am-10pm Tue-Sun*

Sungei Road Laksa $
26 E5
These small but filling bowls of rice noodles in a fragrant curry-like broth are cooked over charcoal for extra depth. Expect to wait 15 to 20 minutes. *9.30am-4pm Thu-Tue*

Swee Choon Tim Sum $
27 D4
Cheap and cheerful, this dim sum joint started as a single shophouse but now takes up four. Its tiny, tasty morsels are a favourite among late-night revellers. *7am-3.30am Wed-Mon*

Vibrant Indian Flavours

Mustard $$
28 A4
A top-tier Indian restaurant on Race Course Rd, specialising in Bengal and Punjab cuisine and known for rich dishes, many cooked with mustard oil. *11.30am-3pm & 6-10.45pm Sun-Fri, 11.30am-4pm & 6-10.45pm Sat*

Lagnaa Barefoot Dining $$
29 B5
Slip off your shoes, choose your spice level (above three is brave) and be treated to homestyle Indian cooking and a chatty host. *11.30am-midnight Tue-Sun*

Sakunthala's $$
30 A3
The fish-head curry is a tangy signature, and the lamb and fish biryani are heady platters of seasoned meat and fluffy rice. *11am-10.30pm*

Gupshup $$$
31 C2
Go on a flavour carousel finessed by Chef Jolly of *MasterChef India* fame in this jewel-box restaurant. The street-snack-inspired entrees are scrumptious. *noon-3pm & 5-10pm Tue-Sun*

Pastas & Pizzas

Cicheti $$$
32 C1
Tuck into contemporary Italian dishes, beautifully charred wood-fired pizzas and made-from-scratch pastas at this slick and buzzing Kampong Glam hot spot. *noon-2.30pm & 6-9.30pm Mon-Fri, 6-10pm Fri & Sat*

Tipo Pasta Bar $$
33 F7
Swoon at the bowls of beautifully handcrafted pasta at this airy and light eatery. Order from

the menu or unleash your creativity by customising your own carb-loaded creation. *11am-10pm*

Locanda $$

34 D4

An intimate hideaway serving Italian classics. You can't go wrong with mains like Secreto Iberico Pork and house-specialty pasta. *noon-3pm & 6-11pm Fri-Sun, 6-11pm Tue-Thu*

Middle Eastern & Mediterranean

Tabbouleh Lebanese Cafe & Restaurant $$

35 B1

This Lebanese eatery is consistently filled with satisfied customers who flock here for the charcoal-grilled meats and mezze – the combo offers a taste of the most popular. *10.30am-midnight*

Beirut Grill $$

36 C2

Indulge in succulent, perfectly charred kebabs at this buzzing restaurant, where a belly dancer enchants guests every Friday and Saturday evening. *11.30am-3.30pm & 5.30-11pm*

Alaturka $$

 C1

Generous sharing plates of Mediterranean and Turkish cuisine; don't miss the moreish lavash bread or the Ispanakli Pide, a boat-shaped flatbread with spinach and cheese. *11.30am-10.30pm*

Byblos $$

38 C1

Bathed in soft blue light, this family-friendly restaurant imports all its ingredients from Turkey and Lebanon, resulting in gloriously fresh and flavourful dishes. *11am-1am*

Vegetarian & Vegan

Komala Vilas $

39 B5

Since 1947, this no-frills eatery has been a staple in Little India, offering authentic and budget-friendly vegetarian South Indian cuisine. Don't miss the wafer-thin *dosa* (lentil-flour pancake). *7am-10.30pm*

MTR 1924 $

40 D1

Join regulars and devour the crispy *dosa* and house speciality *rava idly* (semolina cake with cashews and spices). *8.30am-3pm & 5.30-9.30pm Tue-Sun $*

Kunthaville $$

41 B4

Nibble through a six-course tasting menu rooted in family recipes while seated in a charming classic Colombo tea room. *11am-2pm, 3-5pm & 6-10pm Tue-Sun*

Home-Style Favourites

Hjh Maimunah $

42 E6

Pick and point at dishes to add them to your rice – that's *nasi padang* (rice with curries) for you. The beef rendang is a tender spice bomb. *7.30am-7.30pm Mon-Sat*

Prince Coffee House $

43 B2

Nostalgia hits this 1977 eatery where the original staff still serve their pies and Hainanese pork-chop rice. *11am-8.30pm Wed-Mon*

Blanco Court Prawn Mee $

44 B2

The intense prawn broth is a moreish delight best savoured with yellow noodles for that chewy eggy goodness. *7.30am-4pm Wed-Mon*

Bakes & Cakes

French American Bakery $

45 A1

Follow the irresistible aromas to this bakery on Haji Lane, where French and American-style treats like cakes, cookies and pastries await to tantalise your taste buds. *10am-6pm*

Mother Dough $

 E6

Even before the doors are opened for the day, a queue has quietly formed outside this renowned bakery, coveted for its exquisite pastries – notably the almond croissants. *10am-5pm Tue-Sun*

Lunar Rabbit Bakery $

47 F2

Try to resist the urge to drool over the glowing display case while selecting just one indulgence from the heavenly assortment of artisanal croissants and brioches. *8.30am-5pm Tue-Sun*

Drinking

Hot-Shot Coffee

Chye Seng Huat Hardware

48 F2

Sharp shots and nitro cold brews come with wraps and pasta in this edgy art deco institution with its own roastery. *8.30am-10pm*

Generation Coffee Roasters

 A5

This artisanal-coffee hawker stall in the Tekka Centre bridges the gap between traditional *kopi* and specialty coffee with prices that won't break the bank. *7.30-10.30am & 11.15am-3pm Wed-Sat*

Heap Seng Leong

50 F6

Though dwindling, bulletproof coffee is nothing new in Singapore, this traditional coffee shop has been serving *kopi gu you* (coffee with butter) since 1974. *5am-3pm*

Community Coffee

 F2

Minimalist and oh-so-cool, these kiddos love their light roast and invite you to experiment with their delicious single-origin brews. *9am-6pm Mon-Sat, from noon Sun*

Craft Beers

Druggists

 E2

Beer hounds head to this old-school Chinese medicine hall for its revolving line-up of craft brews. *5pm-midnight Mon, from 4pm Tue-Thu, 11.30am-midnight Fri & Sat, 3-10pm Sun*

Good Luck Beerhouse

 B2

Helping to keep the hip in Haji Lane, this tiny 12-tap beerhouse serves the freshest craft beers from top Singaporean microbreweries. *8am-midnight*

Drinks with Beats

Blu Jaz

 B2

Chilled-out local favourite that pumps with regular live gigs, jam sessions and comedy nights. *11.30am-1.30am Sun-Thu, to 2am Fri & Sat*

Whiskey Library & Jazz Club

 E4

An opulent haven for whiskey aficionados, offering more than 1000 bottles from near and far. Live jazz brings out the vibes on weekends. *5-10pm Tue, Wed & Sun, to midnight Thu-Sat*

Cocktail Dens

Bar Stories

 A1

A menu-free speakeasy; just mention your likes and dislikes and boom! – your perfect cocktail. *5.30-10.30pm Tue-Sun*

Club 5

 F8

Dim, laid-back den with a heavy local influence in its cocktails – why eat chicken rice when you can drink it? *4pm-midnight Mon-Thu, to 2am Fri & Sat, 3-10pm Sun*

Atlas

see 20 D8

Glamorous art deco venue with gilded decor and plush seats. Order a gin-based tipple from the staggering collection. Reserve early. *3pm-midnight Mon, from noon Tue-Thu, noon-2am Fri & Sat*

Shopping

Thrift Bargains

Vintagewknd

58 A2

Step into this Technicolor time capsule straight from the '70s, offering an array of amazing vintage and reworked items. *11am-9pm*

Cartel's Vintage Store

59 B2

One for the lads; rummage through an assortment of new and preloved retro tees, denim jackets, street kicks and accessories. *noon-8pm*

Textiles & Home Decor

Basharahil Bros Batik

60 A1

Discover vibrant batik prints and fabrics, alongside racks of stunning apparel, at one of Singapore's longest-standing batik stores. *10am-6pm Mon-Sat, 12.30-5pm Sun*

Haji Tawakal Carpets

61 B2

Enter this Aladdin's cave, overflowing with statement cushions and carpets – available in traditional and contemporary designs, which the staff are happy to showcase for you. *10am-9pm*

Dilip Textiles

62 B1

A one-stop shop for vibrant block-printed fabrics in various styles. Find napkins, table linen and scarves at affordable prices. *11am-6pm Mon-Sat*

NUKI NUGROHO/SHUTTERSTOCK

Vintagewknd

Scented Journeys

Sifr Aromatics

63 B2

Perfume emporium specialising in custom blends – here you can immerse yourself in a treasure trove of olfactory delights, contemporary or traditional. *11am-8pm Tue-Sat, 11am-5pm Sun & Mon*

Jamal Kazura Aromatics

64 B1

Once dispensing perfumes for those going to Mecca, the expert noses here can recreate contemporary-brand replicas upon request. *9.30am-6pm*

See p108
for eating,
drinking and
shopping
listings

Explore Orchard Road

Researched by Ria de Jong

Now world-famous, Orchard Road began in the 1830s as a dusty, tree-lined track leading to orchards and spice plantations. Nearly a century would pass before it began its transformation into the epitome of modern consumerism we see today.

Following Singapore's rapid post-independence growth, the area boomed with commercial activity and is now home to a vast array of brands, from local designers to international couture. While cultural highlights like the heritage shophouses of Emerald Hill and the presidential residence, the Istana, add historical charm, Orchard Road's heart beats for shopping. You can shop until you drop, pick yourself up and shop some more.

Getting Around

MRT

The Orchard Rd area is serviced by four MRT stations – Orchard Bvld, Orchard Rd, Somerset and Dhoby Ghaut – eliminating the need for an exhaustive walk along its entire length.

Bus

Numerous buses traverse Orchard Rd, which flows in a one-way direction towards the city. Bus stops are found on the left side of the road.

Walking

Should you choose to explore the tree-lined pavement, you'll discover expansive, impeccably maintained paths. If weather conditions pose a challenge, many malls are interconnected via underground walkways.

THE BEST

HERITAGE AREA Emerald Hill Rosd (p104)

HOKKIEN MANSION House of Tan Yeok Nee (p105)

DESIGNER SHOPPING Design Orchard (p106)

HAWKER CENTRE Newton Food Centre (p108)

SHOPPING MALL ION Orchard Mall (p109)

ION Orchard Mall (p109)
2P2PLAY/SHUTTERSTOCK

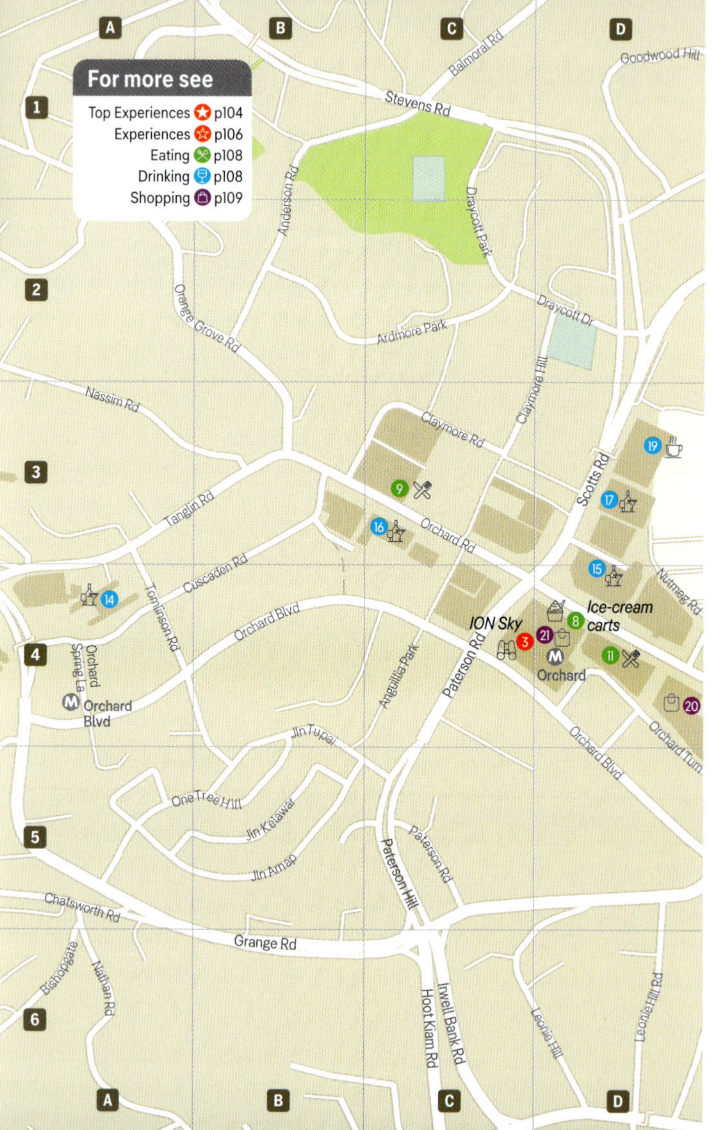
For more see
Top Experiences p104
Experiences p106
Eating p108
Drinking p108
Shopping p109
Stevens Rd
Balmoral Rd
Goodwood Hill
Anderson Rd
Draycott Park
Draycott Dr
Orange Grove Rd
Ardmore Park
Claymore Hill
Nassim Rd
Claymore Rd
Scotts Rd
Tanglin Rd
Orchard Rd
Cuscaden Rd
Tomlinson Rd
Nutmeg Rd
Orchard Blvd
Ice-cream carts
ION Sky
Paterson Rd
Orchard
Anguilla Park
Orchard Spring La
Orchard Blvd
Orchard Turn
Jln Tupai
One Tree Hill
Jln Ketawar
Jln Arnap
Paterson Hill
Paterson Rd
Chatsworth Rd
Grange Rd
Bishopsgate
Nathan Rd
Hoot Kiam Rd
Irwell Bank Rd
Leonie Hill
Leonie Hill Rd

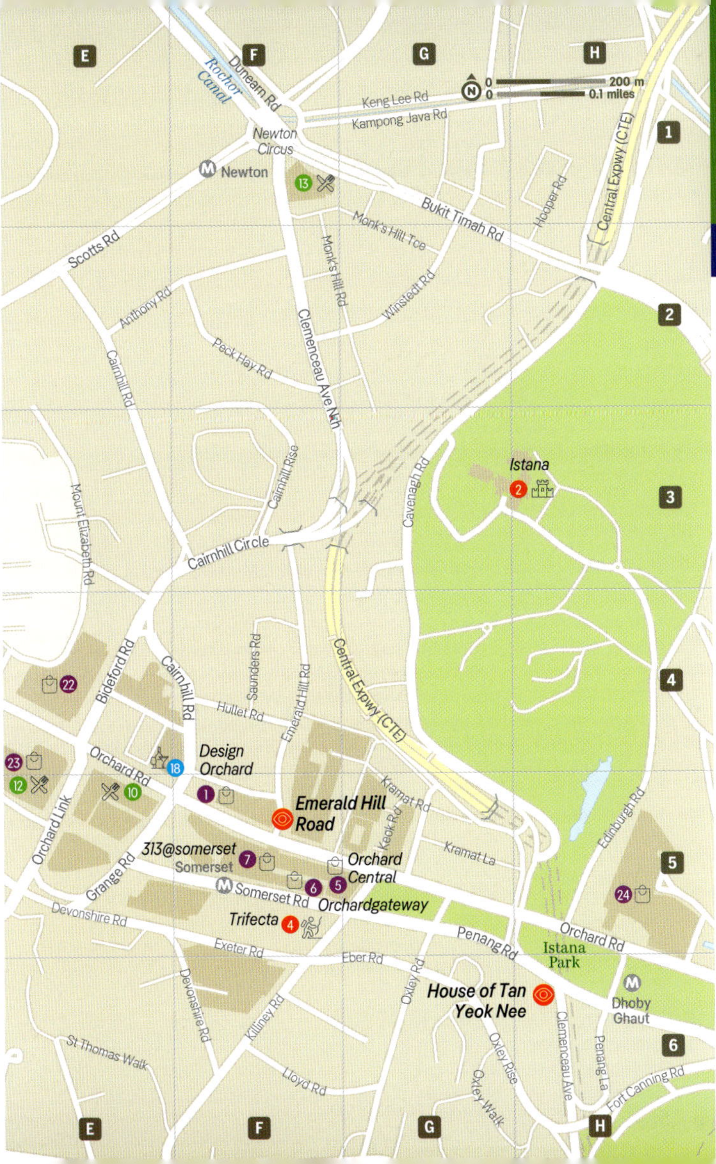

E F G H

0 200 m
0 0.1 miles

1 2 3 4 5 6

Rochor Canal
Dunearn Rd
Keng Lee Rd
Kampong Java Rd
Newton Circus
Newton
13
Bukit Timah Rd
Central Expwy (CTE)
Hooper Rd
Monk's Hill Tce
Monk's Hill Rd
Scotts Rd
Anthony Rd
Winstedt Rd
Peck Hay Rd
Clemenceau Ave Nth
Cairnhill Rd
Cairnhill Rise
Istana
2
Cavenagh Rd
Mount Elizabeth Rd
Cairnhill Circle
Bideford Rd
22
Cairnhill Rd
Saunders Rd
Hullet Rd
Emerald Hill Rd
Central Expwy (CTE)
23
12
Orchard Rd
18
Design Orchard
10
1
Emerald Hill Road
Kramat Rd
Keck Rd
Orchard Link
313@somerset
7
Somerset
Orchard Central
Kramat La
Edinburgh Rd
Grange Rd
6
5
Somerset Rd
Orchardgateway
24
Devonshire Rd
Trifecta
4
Penang Rd
Orchard Rd
Istana Park
Exeter Rd
Eber Rd
Oxley Rd
House of Tan Yeok Nee
Dhoby Ghaut
Devonshire Rd
Killiney Rd
Oxley Rise
Clemenceau Ave
Penang La
St Thomas Walk
Lloyd Rd
Oxley Walk
Fort Canning Rd

★ TOP EXPERIENCE

Emerald Hill Road

The former Peranakan enclave of Emerald Hill Road features beautifully restored shophouses, intricate tiles and shuttered windows. By day, it's perfect for a leisurely stroll; by night, it comes alive with buzzing bars and chilled cafes.

MAP P102 **F5**

PLANNING TIP
You can spend 10 minutes to an hour here, depending on how long you linger. Early morning offers the best photos, when the road is quiet and light soft.

Scan this QR code for the Orchard Heritage Trail, which includes Emerald Hill.

Take in Some Shophouse Beauties

Like much of the surrounding area, Emerald Hill was once filled with spice plantations and orchards before being subdivided into small land parcels and becoming an enclave for wealthy Peranakan and Chinese families. Many of their fine terrace houses still line the street today, showcasing exquisite architectural details. Several are enhanced by Chinese baroque influences evident in their facades, wall embellishments and ceramic floor tiles. Notable examples include **No 56**, one of the oldest buildings, built in 1902; **Nos 39 to 45**, with extensive frontages and a grand Chinese-style entrance gate; and **Nos 120 to 130**, featuring art deco elements from around 1925. Keep an eye out for small metal signs sharing snippets of local history.

Lights, Camera, Action

Emerald Hill Road recently provided the evocative setting for the 2025 Singaporean period drama *Emerald Hill – The Little Nyonya Story*. Set in the 1950s to 1970s, the series follows the intertwined fates of three young Nyonya women from the affluent Peranakan Zhang family living along this historic and picturesque street.

Watering Holes

At the Orchard Road end, century-old shophouses now host lively bars, popular with the after-work crowd thanks to generous happy-hour deals.

★ TOP EXPERIENCE

House of Tan Yeok Nee

The House of Tan Yeok Nee is Singapore's last surviving Grand Mansion; one of the four Chinese-style residences built in the late 1800s by Teochew businessmen. Beautifully restored, it showcases exquisite craftsmanship, vivid carvings and rich symbolism.

MAP P102 **H6**

Treasures Above

The **mansion** *(houseoftyn.sg)* has sweeping swallowtail rooflines and ceiling beams adorned with 24-carat-gold ornaments. Elaborately carved pillars, decorative brackets and intricate latticework showcase exceptional craftsmanship. The roof ridge and gable wall ends feature ceramic art made from broken porcelain shards depicting scenes of longevity and happiness. Inside the entrance hall, the top register of the walls has reinstated secco work illustrating mythical tales, and the historic beams' gold gilding has been carefully restored. The carp-shaped rain spouts are particularly fun.

PLANNING TIP

If your budget allows, secure a reservation at on-site fine-dining restaurant **Loca Niru**, where refined Japanese-French cuisine is served amid the house's stunning interiors for an unforgettable dining experience.

Tricks of the Eye

Fascinating details include the mansion's clever visual tricks. A half-embedded rainwater downpipe is adorned with secco mouldings of flora and fauna, seamlessly blending function with decoration. Above, human figures lean forward, their heads enlarged to appear proportionate from the ground, creating a subtle effect that showcases the craftsmen's skill and playful use of perspective.

Beyond Time Gallery

Explore the mansion's artistry, renovation and historical significance and learn about the family who built it. The animated roofline projection by architect and illustrator Jerome Ng Xin Hao is poignantly beautiful.

Scan this QR code for opening times and to plan your visit.

EXPERIENCES

Discover Singaporean Talent at Design Orchard
DESIGN STORE

MAP: 1 P102 **F5**

Celebrating Singaporean craftsmanship and design innovation in a building conceptualised by renowned homegrown firm WOHA, **Design Orchard** *(designorchard.sg)* is a world-class platform for all things local. **DORS** *(dors.com.sg)* operates the ground floor and brings together 80 brands ranging from beauty products to fashion to home furnishings – this is a great spot to pick up a souvenir of your time in the Lion City. Budding designers populate the 2nd floor's incubation spaces, studios and meeting areas intended to nurture the next generation of Singapore's retail stars. At sunset, head to the roof and watch the shopping and work crowds hot-foot it below.

Visit the Home of the President (If You're Lucky)
PALACE

MAP: 2 P102 **H3**

The official residence of Singapore's president, this neoclassical landmark sits within more than 40 hectares of manicured grounds. Known as the **Istana** *(Malay for 'palace'; istana.gov.sg; adult/child S$20/10)*, the whitewashed building was constructed by the British between 1867 and 1869 as Government House. It was renamed Istana Negara Singapura (Palace of the State of Singapore) when Singapore gained internal self-government in 1959, then shortened to Istana on 9 August 1965, the day the nation became independent from Malaysia, now celebrated annually as National Day. Most visitors only glimpse the heavily guarded gates fronting Orchard Rd, but five times a year these are flung open to welcome the public inside. Open-house days coincide with public holidays; check the website before you set off.

Observe Shoppers from above at ION Sky
VIEWPOINT

MAP: 3 P102 **C4**

If you're feeling high after splashing some moolah at ION Orchard (p109), get even higher at **ION Sky** *(ionorchard.com)*. Perched 56 levels above the city, it delivers jaw-dropping views of Singapore, and on clear days, Malaysia to the north and Indonesia to the south. The ION Sky app lets you identify landmarks through augmented reality. Entry is free from noon to midnight, but visit between noon and 4 pm with a same-day receipt of S$50+ from ION Orchard, and you'll score a complimentary welcome drink (subject to availability). Take the lift from level 4 to reach this sky-high spot.

Swap the Shops for the Slopes at Trifecta
ADVENTURE PARK

MAP: 4 P102 **F5**

If the idea of endless shopping fails to excite you, embark on an adrenaline-pumping experience at

Trifecta *(trifectasingapore.com)*, near Somerset MRT station, instead. This unique destination has mountains, waves and even snow (well, a lifelike surface mimicking snow), allowing you to ski, snowboard, skate and surf all within the urban heart of Singapore.

At the Surf Arena, brace yourself for Asia's grandest standing wave pool, an impressive 9.34m in length and capable of generating waves 60cm deep and towering up to 1.5m. It's an ideal playground for both youthful adventurers (check the minimum age requirements per activity) and those young at heart. There are plenty of introductory classes, but slots fill quickly so book online in advance.

Partake in the Nation's Favourite Pastime

KARAOKE

As you trawl the shopping malls, you'll come across numerous entertainment venues offering KTV – that's karaoke television, for the uninitiated. Here, singing enthusiasts showcase their vocal talents in thematic rooms, complete with state-of-the-art audiovisual systems and (thankfully) soundproofing. You can purchase food and drinks inside, and you pay by the hour. It's always good to check the song lists before heading inside. **Orchard Central** (MAP: 5 P102 **F5**; *fareastmalls.com.sg/orchard-central*), **Orchard-gateway** (MAP: 6 P102 **F5**; *orchardgateway.sg*) and **313@somerset** (MAP: 7 P102 **F5**; *313somerset.com.sg*) malls are hubs for this popular Singaporean hobby.

Savour a Beloved Singaporean Treat

FOOD CART

MAP: 8 P102 **D4**

Amid all the glitz and glamour of Orchard Rd, you'll still spot a few out-of-place-looking, weather-beaten, beach umbrellaed **ice-cream carts** parked by the kerb. Join the queue and savour a beloved local, nostalgic snack: a thick slab of ice cream hugged by a slice of soft, rainbow bread. Pay in cash, then wander on – sticky-fingered, smiling and refreshingly cooled.

ORCHARD ROAD'S FINAL BUILDING BLOCK

Visitors often wonder why the Thai embassy occupies such a large and prominent space amid Orchard Rd's staggeringly expensive real estate. The story goes that back in the 1990s the Thai government was offered S$139 million for the embassy's 17,500-sq-metre plot – but the offer was declined because selling the land would be disrespectful to the memory of the revered King Chulalongkorn (Rama V; 1853–1910), who reportedly picked the land up for a mere S$9000 in the 1890s. And so the embassy remains to this day, newly renovated and drooled over by developers who yearn for its coveted location.

LISTINGS

Best Places for...

$ Budget $$ Midrange $$$ Top End

See p102 for map of locations

Eating

Brunches & Lunches

Merci Marcel $$
9 C3
Breezy outdoor tables are coveted at this French-inspired nosh spot, where a glass of wine pairs beautifully with a French cheese. Book, or arrive before 11.30am. *8am-midnight Tue-Sat, to 11pm Sun & Mon*

Wild Honey $$
10 E5
Longtime Orchard Rd favourite serving excellent all-day breakfasts inspired by all corners of the globe. Book in advance for weekends. *9am-9.30pm Sun-Thu, to 10.30pm Fri & Sat*

Violet Oon $$$
see 21 D4
Elegant Peranakan restaurant serving heritage favourites like dry laksa in a chic, colonial-inspired setting. Plant-based menu available. *noon-10pm*

Hawker Centres & Food Courts

Wisma Atria Food Republic $
11 D4
A cornucopia of street food in air-con comfort. Muck in with the rest of the crowd for seats before joining the longest queues for dishes spanning the globe. *10am-10pm*

Takashimaya Food Village $
12 E5
This expansive food hall in the basement of Takashimaya department store serves Japanese and other Asian culinary classics. *10am-9.30pm*

ION Orchard Food Opera $
see 21 D4
If you need a pit stop while wandering the labyrinthine ION Orchard, head to the basement for upscale local cuisine in colonial heritage surroundings. *10am-10pm*

Newton Food Centre $
 F1
The heaving, smoky open-air courtyard is ringed by more than 100 stalls serving delectable grub. Cash is preferred. *noon-2am, stall times vary*

Drinking

Cocktails & Dance Floors

Manhattan
14 A4
Inspired by the Golden Age, this handsome *Mad Men*–esque bar is an absolute must for aficionados of fine libations. *5pm-midnight Mon-Thu, to 1am Fri & Sat, 6pm-midnight Sun*

Other Room
15 D4
Hidden in the Singapore Marriott's lobby, this speakeasy-style watering hole is the ultimate destination for lively late-night tipples. *6pm-2am Mon-Thu, to 3am Fri & Sat*

Backdrop
 C3
Master bartender Dario Knox shifts away from conventional methods of cocktail creation and

introduces percolated cocktails to the world. *6pm-2am Wed-Thu & Sun, 7pm-3am Fri & Sat*

Brix

 D3

In the Grand Hyatt's basement, this lively, slightly gritty club has a pumping dance floor and live music acts. *9pm-4am Tue-Sat, to 2am Sun & Mon*

Caffeine Hot Spots

Alchemist The Heeren

 F4

Coffee enthusiasts love this minimalistic sip-and-go spot hugging the outside of The Heeren. The pastries are worth the calories. *9am-9pm*

CMCR on the Go @ ION Orchard

see 21 D4

For a quick refuel, stop by for a specialty brew from this small but mighty caffeine powerhouse. *9.30am-9.30pm*

Puzzle Coffee

see 21 D4

Originating from coffee-crazed Melbourne, the brand's inaugural Singaporean outpost brews away in the depths of ION Orchard. *9am-8pm*

Piccolo by Hei Kim

19 D3

A cosy, fuss-free cafe hidden in Far East Plaza, pouring smooth brews with beautifully balanced flavours. *8.30am-5pm Tue-Sun*

Shopping

Best Local Brands

Beyond the Vines

20 D4

The epitome of SG cool, this comprehensive, multidisciplinary design studio offers womenswear, menswear, bags and lifestyle products. Outlets at ION Orchard and Takashimaya. *10am-9.30pm*

In Good Company

see 21 D4

One of Singapore's most lauded home-grown fashion labels known for modern, geometric wardrobe essentials for men and women. *10am-9.30pm*

Benjamin Barker

see 21 D4

Experience the pinnacle of style at the brand's flagship menswear studio in ION Orchard. Discover impeccably tailored suits and shirts, alongside accessories to elevate your dapper ensemble. *10am-10pm*

Le Petit Society

see 22 D4

Stylishly designed, comfortable kids' wear and family collections which blend playful design with quality fabrics. *10am-9pm*

Mega Malls

ION Orchard Mall

21 D4

Futuristic ION is the cream of the Orchard Rd malls. The basement floors focus on mere-mortal high-street labels, while the upper-floor tenants read like an issue of *Vogue*. *10am-10pm*

Paragon

22 E4

Strike a pose inside this Maserati of Orchard Rd malls – all the status labels are here. *10am-10pm*

Ngee Ann City

23 E4

It might look like a forbidding mausoleum, but this marble-and-granite behemoth promises retail giddiness on its seven floors. *10am-9.30pm*

Plaza Singapura

24 H5

The Plaza offers midrange retail and dining options; teens flock here for arcade haven Timezone and a lineup of toy and comic-book shops. *10am-10pm*

See p120
for eating, drinking and shopping listings

Researched by
Ria de Jong

Explore
Holland Village & Dempsey

As Orchard Rd's towering malls gradually give way to soaring rain trees and peaceful greenery, the Singapore Botanic Gardens – the city's green heart and a UNESCO World Heritage Site – steals the spotlight. This lush oasis invites visitors to stroll among tropical plants, tranquil lakes and fragrant blooms. Nearby, leafy Dempsey Hill, once a British Army barracks, now buzzes with stylish art galleries, gourmet grocers, chic boutiques and upscale dining spots perfect for foodies and culture lovers alike. Further west along Holland Rd, vibrant Holland Village offers a lively glimpse into local and expat life with its cosy cafes, trendy shops and lively bars.

Getting Around

MRT

Holland Village and both ends of the Singapore Botanic Gardens are easily accessed from MRT stations (Napier for the Orchard Rd end and Botanic Gardens for the Bukit Timah end).

Bus

Catch bus 7, 75, 77, 105, 106, 123 or 174 on Orchard Blvd to get close to Dempsey Hill (you'll still need to walk up the hill to reach it).

Shuttle

A free shuttle service is available to Dempsey Hill; check the website *(dempseyhill.com/shuttlebusschedule.html)* for timings and pickup locations.

Holland Village (p119)
TANG YAN SONG/SHUTTERSTOCK

THE BEST

GARDEN Singapore Botanic Gardens (p114)

LIFESTYLE PRECINCT Dempsey Hill (p118)

HERITAGE CEMETERY Bukit Brown Cemetery (p117)

NEIGHBOURHOOD MARKET Holland Village (p119)

PERANAKAN RESTAURANT Candlenut (p120)

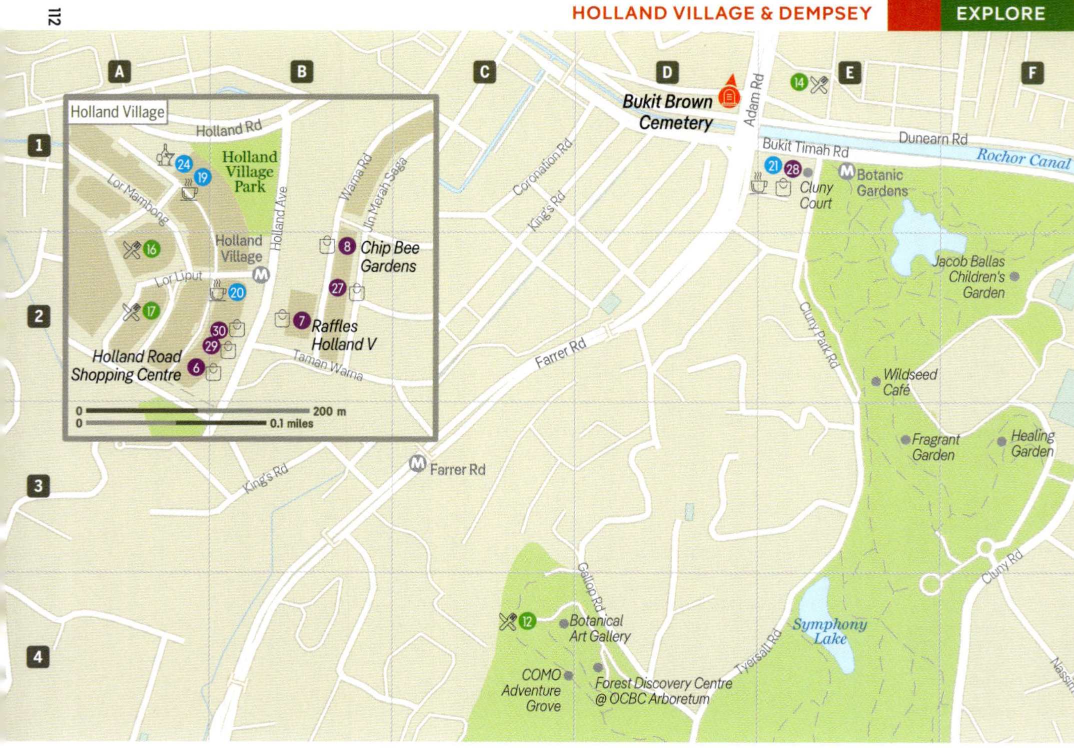
Holland Village
Holland Rd
Holland Village Park
Lor Mambong
Holland Village
Holland Ave
Lor Liput
Holland Road Shopping Centre
Warna Rd
Jln Merah Saga
Chip Bee Gardens
Raffles Holland V
Taman Warna
0 200 m
0 0.1 miles
Coronation Rd
King's Rd
Bukit Brown Cemetery
Adam Rd
Bukit Timah Rd
Dunearn Rd
Rochor Canal
Cluny Court
Botanic Gardens
Jacob Ballas Children's Garden
Cluny Park Rd
Farrer Rd
Wildseed Café
Fragrant Garden
Healing Garden
Evans Rd
Cluny Rd
Symphony Lake
Tyersall Rd
Gallop Rd
Botanical Art Gallery
COMO Adventure Grove
Forest Discovery Centre @ OCBC Arboretum
Nassim Rd

For more see

- Top Experiences p114
- Experiences p118
- Eating p120
- Drinking p121
- Shopping p121

0 500 m
0 0.25 miles

A B C D E F
5 6 7 8

Singapore Botanic Gardens
National Orchid Garden
Halia
Ginger Garden
Learning Forest
Heritage Museum
Swan Lake
Cluny Rd
Lermit Rd
Tasman Serasi
Napier Rd
Tyersall Ave
Holland Rd
Holland Village (550m; see Inset)
Queensway
Ridout Rd
Swettenham Rd
Peirce Rd
Dempsey Rd
Harding Rd
Minden Rd
Sherwood Rd
Camp Rd
Tanglin Rd
Tanglin Hill
Ridley Park
Loewen Rd
TANGLIN

1 Dempsey Hill
2 Ridley Park
3 Museum of Ice Cream
4 Tanglin Gin
5 Gallery26
9
10
11
13
15
18
22
23
25
26

★ TOP EXPERIENCE

Singapore Botanic Gardens

The country's first UNESCO World Heritage Site, the Singapore Botanic Gardens have been a leading hub for plant conservation and research in Southeast Asia since 1875. Visitors are enchanted by its vast expanses of forests, themed gardens, rare orchids and alfresco dining options.

MAP P112 **E5**

PLANNING TIP
The Singapore Botanic Gardens (nparks.gov.sg/sbg) are spread across a massive 82 hectares. Plan your route in advance and prepare to spend at least a whole afternoon or morning here.

Scan this QR code to download a map of the gardens.

National Orchid Garden

Orchids have been bred and cultivated in the **National Orchid Garden** *(pictured; adult/child S$15/free)* since 1928. The 3-hectare space is a showcase of over 1000 species and 2000 hybrids, with around 600 on display at any given time. Descend into the futuristic glass-walled **Tropical Montane Orchidetum**, which simulates the climate in a mountainous forest, before ducking inside the **Tan Hoon Siang Mist House**, a paleotropical garden with highlands conditions. The **VIP Orchid Garden** offers a glimpse into Singapore's unique tradition of orchid diplomacy, showcasing hybrids named after royalty, world leaders and celebrities on display. Be sure to read the information plaques along the trails – they reveal fascinating details about orchid breeding, including Singapore's iconic national flower, the Vanda Miss Joaquim. First cultivated in 1893 by Agnes Joaquim, this resilient hybrid embodies the nation's spirit of strength and perseverance.

Pick a Theme

Embark on an adventure through the world of botany by exploring the themed gardens that showcase a rich tapestry of plant life. Delve into the aromatic wonders of the **Ginger Garden**, housing over 250 Zingiberaceae species, complete

SAB1975/SHUTTERSTOCK

with a hidden waterfall cave and the ginger-centric restaurant **Halia**. Dive into the world of medicinal plants at the **Healing Garden** (closed Tuesday) and learn about their historic remedies. Smell the flowers at the **Fragrant Garden**; aim to visit in the evenings, as this is when the plants' scents are the strongest.

Walk Different Ecosystems

The **Learning Forest** is one of the newest additions to the Botanic Gardens. There are five distinct zones spread over 10 hectares, each easily accessible via elevated walkways and boardwalks. Highlights include the **Keppel Discovery Wetlands**, where you practically walk on the swamp water, and the 8m-high canopy boardwalks in the **SPH Walk of the Giants**. Complete your visit by relaxing in the **Canopy Web**, a spider-like web

QUICK BREAK
Wildseed Café is ideal for a sit-down meal or quick takeaway. For more options, **Cluny Court** outside the Bukit Timah Gate (near Botanic Gardens MRT) has an arsenal of cafes.

OPENING TIMES
The gardens are open from 5am to midnight daily. However, check opening times and closure dates for themed gardens and attractions online. Entry is free, except for the Orchid Garden.

GUIDED TOURS
Free guided tours of the gardens are run every Saturday (except for any fifth Saturday of the month). Register at the service desk.

built into the elevated walkway, listening to the sounds of the forest.

Indoor Activities

Escape the heat by visiting indoor attractions within the gardens. Discover the **Heritage Museum** near the Tanglin Gate, which offers immersive multimedia exhibits detailing the Botanic Gardens' rich heritage and a fascinating look into the past.

At the **Forest Discovery Centre @ OCBC Arboretum**, delve into Singapore's forest ecosystems and the Gardens' historical role in conserving them. The OCBC Arboretum has a growing collection of rare dipterocarps at Gallop House No 5 (Atbara) near the Gallop Gate.

Adjacent, at Gallop House No 7 (Inverturret), explore the **Botanical Art Gallery**, which showcases art's significant role in the scientific documentation of plants in Singapore and the region. The gallery houses Singapore's first permanent display of botanical art.

A Children's World

Those with little ones shouldn't miss the **Jacob Ballas Children's Garden** *(free)* at the northern end of the gardens. The kid-centric green space has nature-themed interactive zones including a sensory garden. Thrill-seekers will love the suspension bridge, treehouse and floating platform. After sweating it out, tiny tots can cool off in the brightly coloured water-play feature. Adults must be accompanied by a child aged 12 or under to enter. The garden is closed Monday.

At the western edge of the gardens lies the **COMO Adventure Grove**, featuring a captivating banyan-tree-inspired structure. Equipped with climbing ropes, hammocks and scenic lookout points, it offers hours of energy-burning excitement for children with swings and a mini obstacle course.

★ TOP EXPERIENCE

Bukit Brown Cemetery

Hidden amid lush greenery, Bukit Brown Cemetery, dating from 1922, is Singapore's largest Chinese burial ground with over 100,000 graves. Overgrown paths reveal elaborately carved tombs telling stories of pioneers. Explore via guided walks, spotting wildlife and glimpsing Singapore's evocative past.

MAP P112 **D1**

Silent Singapore Stories

Step into Singapore's layered past, where moss-covered tombs and twisting roots reveal stories of pioneers and philanthropists. Wander the overgrown trails to discover the grand tomb of Ong Sam Leong, one of the largest in Southeast Asia, and the richly adorned grave of Chew Geok Leong, guarded by stone Sikh sentinels. Don't miss Tan Kheam Hock's unique tomb, which artfully blends Asian and European influences. Wander alone or join a volunteer-led heritage walk (book online), which truly brings these stories to life.

PLANNING TIP
The easiest way to get here is by taxi, or take one of the many buses along Adam Rd (Botanic Garden MRT) that stop near the entrance.

Enter a Sci-Fi World

Look up as you reach the heart of the cemetery to behold towering ancient rain trees draped in moss and vines, creating an otherworldly, Avatar-like canopy. Increasingly popular with photographers and nature enthusiasts, these giants add a haunting beauty to Bukit Brown's historic landscape.

Make Way for the Living

At the *Sounds Of The Earth* installation, wander among 80 unclaimed tombstones exhumed to build the adjacent Lornie Hwy, arranged in elliptical rings that echo footsteps and voices. This quiet memorial prompts reflection on Singapore's balancing act between relentless development and heritage preservation.

Scan this QR code to download a self-guided tour.

EXPERIENCES

Get to Know Dempsey Hill

LEISURE DISTRICT

MAP: 1 P112 **C7**

Once a colonial hill station, **Dempsey Hill** *(dempseyhill.com)* now hides amid lush tropical foliage, dotted with chic brunch spots, beautifully curated art galleries and stylish restaurants that draw in expats and well-heeled locals alike. Compared to neighbouring Holland Village, Dempsey feels quieter, more upmarket and delightfully tucked away – not surprising, given it was once an army barracks.

Previously known as Tanglin Barracks, Dempsey Hill was one of the first British Army barracks constructed in Singapore, built in 1861. Soldiers were housed in spacious, elevated wooden structures topped with thatched *attap* (sugar-palm) roofs. Among the barracks' amenities were hospital wards, washhouses, kitchens, a library, a school and office quarters. The barracks served as the headquarters of the Ministry of Defence between 1972 and 1989, before its current reinvention as an upscale brunch and dining area. The best way to explore? Wander the shaded walkways, linger over artisanal coffee or a decadent brunch, browse designer and artsy finds, then round off your visit with dinner under the canopy of towering trees.

Stroll Ridley Park's Heritage Homes

ARCHITECTURE

MAP: 2 P112 **E8**

At the end of Dempsey Hill's Loewen Rd, you'll come to **Ridley Park**, an estate named in honour of Henry Ridley, the inaugural director of the Singapore Botanic Gardens. A walk down Ridley Park Rd unveils a picturesque ring road, offering glimpses of Singapore's famous black-and-white bungalows. These residences once accommodated British officers overseeing the adjacent barracks but are now leased out to the highest bidder. The expansive gardens that often accompany these homes are highly sought after.

Go Gaga at the Museum of Ice Cream

ENTERTAINMENT ATTRACTION

MAP: 3 P112 **D8**

In vivid contrast to Dempsey Hill's black-and-white aesthetics is the psychedelic pink **Museum of Ice Cream** *(museumoficecream.com/singapore; S$43)*. This dessert-themed wonderland offers a multisensory journey for photo-hungry travellers where you get to play with fun, interactive displays, dive into the largest sprinkle pool in Asia and scoff unlimited ice cream! The flavours are unique, with chendol and lemon yuzu firm favourites. Don't expect a trip here to be educational; it's simply a celebration of unbridled playtime for both grown-ups and little ones.

Discover Distillation at Tanglin Gin

DISTILLERY

MAP: 4 P112 **D7**

For a uniquely Singaporean experience (for those 18 years old and above), venture to **Tanglin Gin** *(tanglin-gin.com; tours from S$49)*, a hidden distillery and bar nestled in leafy Dempsey Hill. Here, gin enthusiasts converge to savour unforgettable flavours. You can embark on a distillery tour or indulge in a cocktail masterclass. Don't miss out on signature tipples like the Orchid Gin, infused with Vanilla planifolia orchid, or the bold Black Powder Gin, tailor-made for the adventurous palate.

Get Revved Up at Gallery26's F1 Exhibition

EXHIBITION

MAP: 5 P112 **D7**

Step into the world of speed at **Gallery26** *(instagram.com/gallery26.dempsey; free)*, an immersive Formula One exhibition in Dempsey Hill. Get up close to legendary Ferrari F1 cars, race memorabilia and parts of the Marina Bay Street Circuit, like 2023 safety barriers. Trace the evolution of the night race, discover race-day engineering secrets, and relive unforgettable moments from 1961 to today. Perfect for a pit stop or an F1 fan's pilgrimage, the experience takes about an hour to explore. It is closed on Monday and Tuesday.

Shop the Holland Village Hood

NEIGHBOURHOOD

Holland Village blends laid-back indie charm with modern retail. Bypass shiny new, pet-friendly One Holland Village mall and head instead to the ageing **Holland Road Shopping Centre** (MAP: 6 P112 **A2**), where upstairs you'll discover art, handicrafts, homewares, nail spas, hair salons and massage joints. Across the road, **Raffles Holland V** (MAP: 7 P112 **B2**) has a handful of fashion boutiques among the eateries. Just behind, **Chip Bee Gardens** (MAP: 8 P112 **B2**) hides indie boutiques, designer homeware stores and artisanal bakeries. Most shops open around lunchtime and stay open until about 9pm.

FROM KAMPONG TO CULTURAL HUB

Once a sleepy *kampong* (village) surrounded by rubber plantations, **Holland Village** blossomed in the 1930s and '40s as the go-to hangout for British servicemen stationed nearby. Locals called it *hue hng au,* meaning 'behind the flower garden' in Hokkien – a nod to its leafy location near the Botanic Gardens. Along Jln Merah Saga, **Chip Bee Gardens** came to life in the 1960s as married quarters for British forces. When the troops departed in the '70s, the neighbourhood transformed: stylish cafes, artisan boutiques and creative studios moved in. Admire the rows of black-and-white terrace houses that lend the area its charm.

LISTINGS

Best Places for...

See p112 for map of locations

$ Budget $$ Midrange $$$ Top End

Eating

Fine Dining

Candlenut $$$
9 C7
This Michelin-starred spot is where Singaporeans bring out-of-towners for a decadent meal of refined Peranakan cuisine. *noon-3pm & 6-10pm*

Burnt Ends $$$

10 C7
Getting a seat is practically impossible, but it's a must-try for barbecue lovers. *noon-2.30pm & 6-11pm Thu-Sat, 6-11pm Tue & Wed*

Min Jiang at Dempsey $$$
11 C7
For the daintiest and most delightful dim sum, book a lunchtime spot at this Dempsey Hill restaurant. *11.30am-2.30pm & 6.30-10.30pm*

Pangium $$$
12 C4
Embark on a delicious journey of refined, Michelin-starred Straits cuisine in a beautiful heritage setting. *noon-1.30pm (last seating) & 6.30-7.30pm (last seating) Thu-Sat, 6.30-7.30pm (last seating) Wed*

Old-School Eats

Samy's Curry Restaurant $$
13 D7
A Singapore institution dishing up superb and affordable Indian cuisine since 1950. Order from the menu or food-display counter; the fish-head curry is outstanding. *11am-3pm & 6-10pm Wed-Mon*

Selera Rasa Nasi Lemak $
14 E1
Locals tout this stall (01-02) as home to the best nasi lemak (coconut rice served with fried anchovies, peanuts and a curry dish) in town. *7am-5pm Mon-Thu, to 3pm Sat & Sun*

Long Beach Seafood $$$

15 D7
Settle in on the veranda, gaze out at the tropical greenery and tackle the cult-status black-pepper crab. *11am-3pm & 5-11.30pm Mon-Fri, 11am-11.30pm Sat & Sun*

Holland Village Food Centre $
16 A2
Beloved local hawker hub dishing out satay, laksa, and *char kway teow* (noodles, clams and eggs) in an unpretentious open-air setting. *10am-10pm*

Sweet Treats

Tai Cheong Bakery $
17 A2
This bakery may have started in Hong Kong, but its egg tarts are much loved on the Little Red Dot. *10am-8.30pm Mon-Thu, to 9pm Fri, 9am-9pm Sat, 9am-8.30pm Sun*

Burnt Ends Bakery $$
18 C7
These irresistible brioche doughnuts are filled with decadence. Arrive early to secure the flavour of your choice. *8am-4pm Thu-Sun*

Drinking

Coffee Spots

Craftsmen Coffee

A1

Sourcing single-origin coffee beans from farms across the globe means this spot pumps out cups of coffee to suit every palate. *8.30am-6pm Sun-Thu, to 10pm Fri & Sat*

Frankie & Fern's

B2

Serving up artisanal coffee, fresh pastries and wholesome brunch fare in a cosy, rooftop location. *9.30am-5.30pm Mon-Thu, to 9.30pm Fri-Sun*

MICRO | bakery

E1

Just outside the gardens at Serene Centre, this tiny hole-in-the-wall bakery is pure heaven for bread and coffee lovers. *8am-4pm Wed-Sun*

Alcoholic Tipples

RedDot Brewhouse

D7

This is a local favourite for microbrews in the jungle, including an eye-catching, spirulina-spiked green lager. *11.30am-10pm Mon, to 10.30pm Tue-Thu & Sun, to 11pm Fri & Sat*

Dempsey Cookhouse & Bar

D7

This swanky bar, inside the Dempsey Cookhouse, concocts delectable cocktails in a buzzy atmosphere. Monday is martini night. *6-11.30pm Sun-Thu, to midnight Fri & Sat*

Le Bon Funk

A1

A European wine bar in the tropics. Order a glass from one of Singapore's best-curated menus of natural wines. Counter or window seats are prime spots. *5-10pm Tue-Fri, from noon Sat & Sun*

Shopping

Designer Threads

Dover Street Market

25 D7

By Comme des Garçons designer Rei Kawakubo and her husband, this concept store is full of luxury fashion brands and streetwear labels. *11am-8pm*

Kids 21 Dempsey

D7

Kit your kids from head to toe in designer duds and accessories at this emporium curated for the under-12 cool crowd. *11am-8pm*

Atelier Ong Shunmugam

B2

The shop of Priscilla Shunmugam, one of Singapore's top up-and-coming designers, is as stunning as her modern interpretations on Asian dresses. *noon-7pm Tue-Sat by appt*

rue Madame

E1

Parisienne chic meets Singapore heat at this beautifully curated boutique filled with European brands at neighbourhood shopping hub Cluny Court. *10am-9pm*

Singapore Souvenirs

Independent Market

29 B2

Quirky and well-designed Singaporean themed gifts and homewares. The shop assistants can enlighten you with regards to the Singaporean humour. *10am-7.30pm*

Lim's Holland Village

30 B2

Asian-inspired homewares and furniture pieces, from Chinese wedding cabinets to fashionable ginger-jar lamps. Most pieces are new (no antiques), and well-priced. *10am-8pm*

See p134
for eating,
drinking and
shopping
listings

Explore
Eastern Singapore

Researched by
Morgan Awyong

Singapore's eastern coastline was once characterised by *kampongs* (villages), mango swamps, coconut plantations and holiday bungalows for wealthy city folk. The landscape transformed drastically with the 1962 East Coast land reclamation. Today, the eastern neighbourhoods offer a window into Singaporean culture. Closest to the city is **Geylang**, formerly a red light district, which now thrives with temples and mosques. To the east, **Joo Chiat** with its multicoloured shophouses represents the heart of the Peranakan community. East Coast Park offers endless recreational activities along the seafront. Furthest east lies **Changi**, home to the poignant Changi Museum and a gateway to Pulau Ubin via bumboats (motorised sampans).

Getting Around

MRT

Together with the older MRT East-West and Downtown Lines, the new Thomson-East Coast Line has made travelling to Eastern Singapore a breeeze.

Bus

To head out to Changi Village and Changi Chapel & Museum, get on bus 2 from Tanah Merah MRT.

Taxi

Although the MRT and bus services now have this section of the island covered, you may still need to use a taxi to shuttle between locations.

Peranakan terrace houses (p130)
JUSTIN ADAM LEE/SHUTTERSTOCK

THE BEST

A
B
C
D
1
2
3
4
5
6
Aljunied
Paya Lebar
GEYLANG
Sims Ave
Geylang East Ave 2
Paya Lebar Rd
Lorong 31
Lorong 33
Lorong 35
Geylang Rd
Lorong 27
Lorong 29
Masjid Khadijah
Yong He Eating House
Lorong 22
Lorong 24A
Lorong 28
Guillemard Rd
Geylang River
Tanjong Katong Rd
Dunman Rd
Dakota
Old Airport Rd
PUNGGOL
Selat Johor (Strait of Johor)
Pulau Ubin
Changi Point Coastal Walk
Serangoon Harbour
PASIR RIS
Loyang Tua Pek Kong Temple
Changi Village
Tampines Expwy (TPE)
TAMPINES
Jewel
Changi Chapel & Museum
Singapore Changi Airport
Bedok Reservoir
Pan Island Expwy (PIE)
BEDOK
East Coast Pkwy (ECP)
Strait of Singapore
0 2 km
0 1 miles
Crescent Rd
Goodman Rd
Branksome Rd
Wilkinson Rd
Bournemouth Rd

E
F
G
H
0 500 m
0 0.25 miles
For more see
Top Experiences p126
Experiences p130
Eating p134
Drinking p136
Shopping p137
1
2
3
4
5
6
Sims Ave
Changi Rd
Geylang Serai Heritage Gallery
Intan
Joo Chiat Tce
Joo Chiat Pl
Joo Chiat La
Mangis Rd
JOO CHIAT (KATONG)
Still Rd
See Inset
Onan Rd
Carpmael Rd
Crane Rd
Haig Rd
Tembeling Rd
Joo Chiat Rd
Everitt Rd
Koon Seng Rd
Ceylon La
Eurasian Heritage Gallery; Quentin's
Straits Enclave
Peranakan terrace houses
Dunman Rd
Duku Rd
Katong Antique House
Jago Cl
Chapel Rd
Sea Ave
Cheow Keng Rd
East Coast Rd
Ceylon Rd
Marshall Rd
Fowlie Rd
Sri Senpaga Vinayagar Temple
Brooke Rd
Marine Parade Rd
Mountbatten Rd
Amber Gardens
Amber Rd
Tanjong Katong Rd
East Coast Park
Strait of Singapore

★ TOP EXPERIENCE

Changi Chapel & Museum

Although shifted from the original Changi prison site in 2001, the haunting Changi Chapel & Museum remains a powerful ode to the courage of the civilian internees and WWII Allied prisoners of war (POWs) who were interned here during the Japanese occupation of Singapore.

MAP P124 **B5**

PLANNING TIP
Take the MRT Downtown Line to Upper Changi station, then bus 2. Alight seven stops later at stop number 97201 opposite Changi Chapel & Museum and cross the road to the museum.

Scan the QR code to download the visitor guide and book tickets.

The Museum

Through eight zones, the **museum** *(heritage.sg/changichapelmuseum; adult/child under 6 S$9/free)* chronicles the internees' harrowing experiences through personal artefacts, interactive displays, photographs and gripping accounts. A poignant highlight is the replica Changi prison cell, complete with an authentic door. Built for one, these cells were used for up to four prisoners. Visitors can hear historical recordings of conversations between internees through speakers in the cell. Resourcefulness and determination are evident in the Morse-code transmitter tucked inside a matchbox and the patchwork quilts made by women internees, which concealed secret codes decipherable only by loved ones.

Changi Murals

The museum is also home to remarkable full-size replicas of the famous Changi murals painted by POW Stanley Warren in the old POW hospital. The original murals, located in Block 151 of the nearby Changi Army Camp, are inaccessible to the public.

Changi Chapel

A replica of the Changi Chapel, originally built by inmates as a focus for worship and a sign of solidarity, stands as the museum's centrepiece. Here, visitors can find the Changi Cross, crafted in 1942 using the casing of a 4.5in howitzer shell and brass strips sourced from camp workshops.

★ TOP EXPERIENCE

Pulau Ubin

Across the seas from Changi Village, Pulau Ubin (Granite Island) seems worlds apart from mainland Singapore. Singaporeans like to wax nostalgic about Ubin's *kampong* (village) atmosphere, and it remains a rural, unkempt expanse of jungle full of wildlife and secret shrines.

A Short Sail Away

Set aside a full day to explore, and bring cash and insect repellant. The only way to and from the **island** *(pulau-ubin.nparks.gov.sg)* is by small bumboats from Changi Village, running from 6am to 6pm. They depart when there are 12 passengers gathered. A one-way 15-minute ride costs S$4 per person. When you arrive, hire a bicycle from the main village and take to the trails.

Eastern Wetlands

Typical wooden village houses dot the eastern routes. At the far end, you can explore Chek Jawa Wetlands, with the 1km Chek Jawa Boardwalk and 20m-high Jejawi Tower. You'll find wildlife in abundance including crabs in the water, oriental pied hornbills flying by, or small wild pigs in the forest.

Western Quarries & Shrines

To the west are some viewing points over the disused quarries, including one from atop Puaka Hill. Locals pray at the serene Wei Tuo Fa Gong Temple with prayer flags fluttering over a turtle-filled pond, and the enigmatic German Girl Shrine which is said to grant lottery luck. While cycling, you'll find few refreshment stands besides Ah Ma Drink Stall. However, there are some places to get *zi char* (family-style sharing) dishes and seafood near the pier.

MAP P124 **B4**

PLANNING TIP
Start early and take the MRT East–West line to Tanah Merah station, then bus 2. Alight at Changi Village and head to the jetty.

Scan the QR code for park details and a map.

Walk Joo Chiat

Joo Chiat (part of Katong) is best seen on foot, so that you can admire the architecture and street art, and duck into the area's independent boutiques and cafes. The mix of contemporary and traditional businesses exemplifies Singapore's knack for merging heritage with modernity.

START	END	LENGTH
Geylang Serai Market	328 Katong Laksa	2.4km; 2½hr

1 A Village-Inspired Market

Start your adventure at **Geylang Serai Market & Food Centre** (p134), which is the heart of Singapore's Malay community. Explore the lively wet market and hawker stalls before crossing Changi Rd and heading south down Lor 101 Changi.

2 Peranakan Culture

Take a left onto Joo Chiat Tce and walk past a stunning row of heritage shophouses. If you have time, plan ahead and book a tour at the **Intan** (p130), a private museum on this street. Turn right at Everitt Rd and continue south to Joo Chiat Pl. Pop into **Chip Guan Heng** and ask for an old-school *potong* (cut) ice lolly for S$1.

3 A Dose of Temple Luck

Turn left down Tembeling Rd to the ornate Buddhist **Kuan Im Tng Temple** and rub the belly of the jolly Maitreya Buddha for good luck. Continue your way down Tembeling Rd.

4 A Perfectly Pastel Street

Have your camera at the ready when you reach **Koon Seng Road** to capture the beautiful pastel **Peranakan terrace houses** (p130). Most are private residences so be respectful when taking pictures.

5 Where Old-School Meets New

Photographed out, continue down Joo Chiat Rd to discover rattan haven **Teong Theng Co**, a Joo Chiat stalwart since 1945. Gentrification is in full swing here, so there are plenty of hip coffee spots and funky boutiques like **Cat Socrates** (p137) to spend some time in the area.

6 Enter a Peranakan Wonderland

Continuing south along Joo Chiat Rd, turn right when you reach East Coast Rd to find bright-blue shophouse **Rumah Bebe**, purveyor of all things Peranakan along with neighbour **Kim Choo Kueh Chang** (p134).

7 A Colourful Temple

Stroll further along and turn at Ceylon Rd to take in the beauty of the **Sri Senpaga Vinayagar Temple** (p132), whose interior contrasts the yellow-and-clay coloured exterior with wonderful colourful devotional art.

8 Iconic Chow

Finally, double back to the street corner and pull up a seat at **328 Katong Laksa**. Dive into a creamy rich noodle dish for a bowl of lip-smacking cult-status goodness.

EXPERIENCES

Dive into Peranakan Heritage

MUSEUMS

Nestled on Joo Chiat Tce, private-residence-museum the **Intan** (MAP: 1 P124 **F2**; *the-intan.com; adult/child S$64.20/32.10*) offers a range of Peranakan experiences. Owner Alvin Yapp warmly welcomes visitors and shares candid stories behind his three decades' worth of Peranakan antiques, artefacts and textiles, all tucked away on the no-photos-allowed 2nd floor. Treat yourself to the Tea Experience, where you can savour delightful Nonya *kueh* (bite-sized snacks) while regaled by the spritely polyglot.

The lifelong passion of late Mr Peter Wee, founder and fourth-generation Peranakan, **Katong Antique House** (MAP: 2 P124 **H4**; *instagram.com/katongantiquehouse; S$15*) on East Coast Rd is filled with painstakingly curated items, from photographs to jewellery. The museum is now lovingly maintained by its new guardians who strive to preserve Mr Wee's dream and heritage.

For walk-ins, there's **Straits Enclave** (MAP: 3 P124 **F3**; *singaporeperanakanmuseum.com; S$12*) acting as museum and costume-rental shop. Discover Baba-Nonya culture through an incredible collection of colourful antiques and artefacts. Don't miss the 150-year-old bed, perfectly laid out for a traditional Peranakan wedding.

Stroll the Picture-Perfect Koon Seng Road

ARCHITECTURE

MAP: 4 P124 **G3**

Koon Seng Rd is lined with extraordinary **Peranakan terrace houses** and is arguably Singapore's most colourful and photographed street. These multicoloured beauties contrast from unit to unit, and are joyously adorned with an assortment of stucco dragons, birds and crabs. A feature of this style of architecture is the *pintu pagar* (swinging doors) at the dwellings' front entrances, which let in refreshing cross-breezes and ensure privacy. What makes them quintessentially Peranakan is their fusion of design influences; with bat-shaped vents from the Chinese, timber roof eaves and balustrades from the Malays, and brilliantly glazed European tiles. Nowadays, most terrace houses serve as private homes, which is worth keeping in mind when you visit the area to take pictures.

Discover the Sacred & Secular in Geylang

NEIGHBOURHOOD

All those salacious rumours about Geylang being peppered with brothels, girly bars and dubious hotels are absolutely accurate. A nocturnal stroll along its streets reveals a pretty risqué ambience – at least by Singaporean standards. Yet, strange as it may seem, Geylang is also one of the Lion City's spiritual hubs with numerous temples, mosques, religious schools and shrines. **Masjid Khadijah**

(MAP: 5 P124 B2; *khadijahmosque.org; free*) is unmissable with its minarets along the main stretch, and several fetching *lorongs* (alleys) well worth checking out during a daytime stroll include **Lorong 27** (MAP: 6 P124 A2) and **Lorong 29** (MAP: 7 P124 B2), where decorated Buddhist, Taoist and Hindu temples sit side by side.

Geylang's other blessing is its food scene. Geylang Rd and Sims Ave teem with cheap, tasty, unceremonious local eateries. If you're feeling adventurous, treat yourself to a bowl of frog porridge at **Geylang Lor 9 Fresh Frog Porridge** (MAP: 8 P124 A2; *geylanglor9.com*) or settle for fried fritters and silky beancurd at **Yong He Eating House** (MAP: 9 P124 A2; *yonghetoast.com*).

Learn about Geylang's Heritage

HERITAGE MUSEUMS

Embark on a journey through Geylang's history by visiting two small yet enriching museums. Begin at the **Geylang Serai Heritage Gallery** (MAP: 10 P124 E1; *free*), which traces the district's evolution from a lemongrass plantation to a vibrant residential estate. Discover its changing charm through captivating exhibits, including photographs, recordings and books.

Next explore the **Eurasian Heritage Gallery** (MAP: 11 P124 F3; *eurasians.sg/our-heritage-gallery; S$5*), where the unique story of the Eurasian community unfolds. Despite constituting less than 1% of the population, their East-meets-West heritage profoundly influences Singapore's cultural landscape. Delve into their remarkable history, achievements and vibrant traditions spanning religion, cuisine, music and sports. A section on notable figures includes Joseph Schooling, the national swimming champion who won Singapore its first ever Olympic gold medal. To savour the delightful flavours of Eurasian cuisine, make your way to **Quentin's** (see 11 P124 F3; *quentins.com.sg*),

WHO ARE THE PERANAKANS?

In Singapore, Peranakan (locally born) people are descendants of immigrants who married local women mainly of Malay origin. The result of hundreds of years of immersion and the meeting of foreign and local customs has resulted in an intriguing hybrid culture that's experiencing a revival. It's acknowledged that the Peranakan fall into three broad categories. The Chitty Melaka and Jawi Peranakan are descended from Indian migrants, while the Straits Chinese Peranakan – Singapore's largest group – are of mainland Chinese origin. The rich tapestry of heritage and customs comes to life in a captivating display, either retold by its keepers at the private museums in Katong, or the official Peranakan Museum (p51) on Armenian St.

located on the ground floor of the same building.

Enjoy a Day by the Sea in East Coast Park

PARK

MAP: 12 P124 H6

East Coasters' communal backyard, the 15km stretch of seafront known as **East Coast Park** *(nparks.gov.sg)* is where Singaporeans come to swim, windsurf, wakeboard, kayak, picnic and bike. You'll find swaying coconut palms, patches of bushland, a lagoon, sea-sports clubs and some excellent eating options. Kid-friendly playgrounds abound, while bike hire is conveniently scattered along the shoreline. No visit here is complete without indulging in smoky satay and seafood at seaside East Coast Lagoon Food Village (p134) . Take the MRT to Marine Parade station and dodge into the Marine Parade Underpass to start your beach break.

Visit the Glorious Sri Senpaga Vinayagar Temple

HINDU TEMPLE

MAP: 13 P124 G4

One of the most beautiful Hindu temples in Singapore, yellow-and-clay coloured **Sri Senpaga Vinayagar Temple** *(ssvt.org.sg; free)* is notable for its *kamala paatham,* a specially sculpted granite foot stone found in certain ancient Hindu temples. Adding to the building's grandeur is the inner sanctum, which features a lavish roof adorned with a resplendent layer of gold. Your eyes will dart to either the beautifully painted ceiling frescos from Hindu mythology or the show-stopping 4.5m golden centrepiece. The latter was built at a cost of S$200,000 and is Southeast Asia's first musical pillar, producing different melodic notes when tapped. There is also colourful devotional art around the compound accompanied by labels in a range of languages.

Admire the Religious Melting Pot of Loyang Tua Pek Kong Temple

TEMPLE

MAP: 14 P124 B4

Loyang Tua Pek Kong Temple *(lytpk.org.sg; free)* has its origins in the 1980s, when a simple hut was constructed to house statues of Taoist, Buddhist and Hindu deities discovered near the Loyang coastline. Unfortunately, a fire in 1996 devastated the shrine, leading to the construction of a temple at Loyang Way before the institution moved to its current location in 2007. Today, this contemporary temple showcases impressive wooden carvings, intricate designs of swirling dragons, and hundreds of colourful effigies depicting deities, gods and saints. It represents the inclusive Singaporean approach to spirituality, bringing together three religions – Hinduism, Buddhism and Taoism – under one vast roof. There's even a shrine dedicated to Datuk Kung, a revered figure in Malay mysticism and Chinese Taoist traditions.

Enjoy Sea Breezes in Changi Village

NEIGHBOURHOOD

On the far northeast coast, **Changi Village** (MAP: 15 P124 C4) is a welcome respite from the city's commotion. It's a more laid-back side to Singapore, where locals embrace the comfort of sleeveless T-shirts, board shorts and flip-flops. While the low-slung buildings are modern, the atmosphere exudes a village-like charm, with the lively Changi Village Hawker Centre (p134) the focal point. Foodies flock here for the three nasi lemak (coconut rice) stalls – **Missy Corner** (01-26), **International Muslim Food Stall Nasi Lemak** (01-03) and **Changi Famous Nasi Lemak** (01-28) – sparking endless debates about the best version.

Adjacent to the hawker centre is the **Changi Point Ferry Terminal** (MAP: 16 P124 C4), where you can catch bumboats to Pulau Ubin or Malaysia's Desaru Coast. Just behind is the starting point for the **Changi Point Coastal Walk** (MAP: 17 P124 C4), a breezy 2.2km-long boardwalk leading past mangroves, a sandy beach and the verdant grounds of government holiday villas.

Linger at the Airport for Jewel

SHOPPING MALL

MAP: 18 P124 C5

If you're travelling through Changi Airport, save some time to explore the architecturally awe-inspiring **Jewel** *(jewelchangiairport.com)*, accessible only on the land side. The lifestyle mall boasts top-notch restaurants, local and global retailers, a cinema, spas and even a hotel. At its heart, looking like the set of *Jurassic Park* thanks to its cascading gardens, is the 40m-high waterfall that descends from the glass-dome ceiling, from 10am to 10pm daily. The world's largest indoor waterfall, the **Jewel Rain Vortex** will take your breath away, and even more so when a public light-and-music showcase heightens its beauty at 8pm and 9pm Mondays to Thursdays, with an additional 10pm show on weekends.

THE KING OF FRUIT

Durians get a bad rap in Singapore. They're banned from nearly all public transport (most notably the MRT), few hotels allow them through their doors, and many shopping malls enforce a 'no durians' policy. Why? Well, they're really, really pungent. However, many Singaporeans adore them, so you should at least try one. You'll find several street-side stalls with tables for feasting at the city end of Sims Ave. The sellers will happily advise which to pick and how to eat it. Use the offered gloves, or your hands will stink for days.

LISTINGS

Best Places for...

$ Budget $$ Midrange $$$ Top End

See p124 for map of locations

Eating

Peranakan Flavours

Guan Hoe Soon $$
19 F2
Singapore's oldest Peranakan restaurant, established in 1953. Try the classic *ayam buah keluak* (chicken stewed with dark nuts). *11am-3pm & 5.30-9pm*

Old Bibik's Peranakan Kitchen $$
20 G3
Time-honoured recipes that bring back faithful customers. The beef rendang melts in your mouth. *11.30am-9.30pm*

Peranakan Inn & Lounge $$
21 H4
Classics like Nonya *chap chye* (mixed vegetables) and *kueh pie tee* (cooked turnip and shrimp in a crunchy pastry shell) are tops here. *11am-3pm & 6-10pm*

Kim Choo Kueh Chang $
22 G4
Traditional Nonya *kueh* and rice dumplings since 1945. The *ondeh ondeh* (sweet *pandan* rice-cake ball) and the *kueh dadah* (*pandan* crepes with coconut and palm sugar) are top picks. *9am-9pm*

Hawker Centres

East Coast Lagoon Food Village $
23 A6
A breezy beachside hawker centre with plenty of hawker staples such as satay, laksa and stingray. *11am-10pm; stall times vary*

Old Airport Road Food Centre $
 B3
You'll find many 'die, die, must try' dishes in this behemoth hawker centre with an army of over 150 stalls. *6am-10.30pm; stall times vary*

Changi Village Hawker Centre $
see 15 C4
Seaside centre with numerous highly praised nasi lemak (coconut rice) stalls. Come to discover your favourite. *6am-midnight Mon-Fri, 24hr Sat & Sun; stall times vary*

Geylang Serai Market & Food Centre $
25 E1
Suitably inspired by *kampong* (village) architecture, this bustling market is filled with Malay and Indian stalls; it's a good spot for *nasi padang* (rice with curries). *7am-10pm; stall times vary*

Heritage Haunts

Chin Mee Chin Confectionery $
26 H4
This refreshed century-old heritage bakery still pumps out old-style coffee and bakes. The house-made *kaya* (coconut jam) is a treat. *8am-4pm Tue-Sun*

Sin Heng Claypot Bak Koot Teh $
27 G4
Peppery or herbal? Both versions bathe tender pork ribs in bubbling rich broth made smoky with claypots. *10am-11.30pm Tue-Sun*

Janggut Laksa $

28 G4

The laksa here is unctuous, aromatic and a tad sweet. *10.30am-4.30pm*

Kway Guan Huat Joo Chiat Popiah $

29 F2

This 1938 institution adds a fried-fish crisp twist to their slow-cooked turnip rolls, wrapped in chewy, handmade skin. *9am-2pm Tue-Sun*

Legendary Seafood Classics

No Signboard Seafood $$

30 A2

Originating as an unnamed hawker stall in the 1970s, this restaurant is famous for white pepper and chilli crab. *11am-12.15am*

Hua Yu Wee Seafood $$

31 B6

Serves traditional *zi char* (family-style sharing) dishes in a rambling bungalow. It's informal, bustling and a true Singaporean experience. *5-11pm*

Roland Restaurant $$

32 H5

According to Roland, it was his mum, Mrs Lim, who invented Singapore's iconic chilli crab in the 1950s. *11.30am-2.30pm & 6-10pm*

Mediterranean & Italian

Al Forno $$

33 A6

This casual Italian eatery is an East Coast institution that has served loyal customers hearty meals since 1995. Don't miss the thin-crust wood-fired pizzas. *11.30am-2pm & 6-10pm Mon-Thu, 11.30am-2pm & 5.30-10pm Fri-Sun*

Forma $$$

34 G3

Savour the essence of rural Italy with fresh handmade pasta and hearty mains, capturing the authentic flavours of traditional Italian cuisine. *6-10.30pm Tue-Thu, noon-2.30pm & 6-10.30pm Fri-Sun*

Blu Kouzina $$

35 A6

With plenty of Greek-island vibes (it's just missing the sea), this charming taverna is renowned for fresh dips, salads and perfectly grilled meats. *11.30am-3.30pm & 5.30-10.30pm*

Fico $$$

36 B6

Experience seaside dining reminiscent of Puglia with a seasonal menu crafted for sharing: handmade pastas, succulent seafood and Focaccina – focaccia and pizza's lovechild. *5.30-10.30pm Mon-Wed, 11.30am-3pm & 5.30-10.30pm Thu, 11.30am-10.30pm Fri-Sun*

Casual Cafes

PS.Cafe East Coast Park $$

37 A6

Take a seat either indoors or outdoors and enjoy the black-and-white breezy beach feels with stellar water views, food and coffee. *8am-10pm Sun-Thu, to 10.30pm Fri & Sat*

Supernova $$

38 E4

With ample seating, this place creates a real buzz, thanks to its excellent caffeine hits and hearty breakfasts. Nights bring cocktails and natural wines. *8am-7pm Sun-Wed, to 10pm Thu-Sat*

Hello Arigato $$

39 F3

Indulge in Japanese-inspired comfort food, specialty coffee and delectable bakes at this lifestyle cafe renowned for its mouthwatering Japanese-style *sando* (sandwiches) and irresistible twister fries. *9am-5pm Tue-Sun*

June Coffee $$

 G4

If you like flavoured coffee and pasta, this lively spot serves sesame lattes, *kinako* (soya-bean powder) matchas and honey babycinos. *10.30am-6.30pm Mon-Wed, 10am-7pm Fri & Sat, 10.30am-6pm Sun*

Sweet Treats

Petit Pain $

 F2

Join the snaking queue outside this bakery, where the coveted viennoiseries are released thrice daily. They're soft, buttery, flaky – in short, divine. *10.30am-2.30pm Thu-Sun*

Birds of Paradise $

 G4

Not your run-of-the-mill ice-cream shop, this is more a high-end boutique stocked with botanical gelatos – all using natural ingredients like fruits, flowers, herbs and spices. *noon-10pm Sun-Thu, to 10.30pm Fri & Sat*

Ecstatic Desserts $

 F2

Pillowy soft mochi and ice-cold dessert soups should be your natural response to the hot weather outside, especially when they're this good. *11.30am-9pm Wed-Mon*

Drinking

Serious Coffee

174Bingo

 F2

Like stepping into a craftsman's living room, fresh careful brews here come with toothsome bakes like the pistachio tart and cherry pie – often selling out. *8.30am-4.30pm Wed-Fri, to 5.30pm Sat & Sun*

Cata Coffee

 F2

Sip a darn good brew under a rainbow at this balmy joint. The standing tables are perfect for those on the go. *8am-4pm*

Common Man Coffee Roasters

 F2

All-day brunching at its finest. It has a coffee academy and its own roastery – good coffee is a given. *7.30am-9.30pm Tue-Sun, to 5pm Mon*

Kings Cart Coffee Factory

47 G3

If you're serious about coffee, this is the place for you. For something different, try one of its 'Singapore Signature' coffees. *9am-6pm*

After-Dark Drinks

Freebird

 F5

Chill out at this craft-beer haven with 12 rotating taps and a fully stocked fridge. On weekends, the outdoor courtyard comes alive with DJ beats. *3pm-midnight Tue-Fri, from 2pm Sat & Sun*

60ml by Asador

 F2

Step into a sultry speakeasy tucked behind a mirror at Asador restaurant. The cocktails here pack a punch with generous 60ml pours, reflecting the bar's fittingly bold name. *5.30pm-midnight*

Hidden Story

 G4

Concealed behind a freezer door, this Prohibition-style bar's exemplary cocktail list pays homage to the neighbourhood's rich Peranakan heritage. *5pm-midnight Mon-Sat*

Winery Gourmet Bar

 A6

This cosy bar is a haven for Old World wine aficionados, featuring an extensive collection from Europe including rare finds from far-flung regions. *3pm-midnight Mon-Fri, from noon Sat, noon-10pm Sun*

Shopping

Lifestyle & Fashion Boutiques

Sojao

52 F3

The organic cotton bedlinen and loungewear are buttery soft and come in chic sophisticated colours that make bedtime a luxurious indulgence. *11am-7pm*

Tiger & Lotus

53 G3

Dreamy shop curating a selection of designer homewares; some whimsical, others luxurious, all begging to come home with you. *10.30am-6.30pm*

Cat Socrates

54 G4

Complete with a friendly feline 'assistant shopkeeper', this eclectic boutique is filled with wares from independent local and foreign designers. *10am-7pm Tue-Fri & Sun, to 7pm Mon, to 8pm Sat*

Rye

55 F2

A Singapore-based womenswear label presenting transitional capsule collections, featuring pared-down and timeless pieces perfect for effortlessly elegant style statements. *11am-7pm Mon-Fri, from 10.30am Sat & Sun*

Vintage Finds

RetroCrates

56 G4

Independent store specialising in pre-owned vinyl and new records, assisted by seasoned audiophile staff. *noon-6pm Tue-Fri, from 11am Sat, noon-5pm Sun*

A Vintage Tale

57 F3

A wonderfully eclectic vintage store bursting with brightly coloured treasures, from dresses and bags to jewellery, carefully curated from around the world. *11.30am-6.30pm Tue-Thu, to 7.30pm Fri & Sat, noon-6pm Sun*

Echo Vintage

58 G3

Like hunting at a flea market – pick up some finished pieces or create your own jewellery with their charms. *10am-9.30pm*

Tasty Souvenirs

Rich & Good Cake Shop

see 18 C5

A comforting classic, these swiss rolls keep it simple with quality ingredients, including slowcooked *pandan kaya* (coconut jam), a Singaporean signature. *10am-10pm*

Bee Cheng Hiang

see 18 C5

Glistening sheets of barbecued pork jerky or cotton-candy-like pork floss? The only answer: get both! *10am-10pm*

Kwong Cheong Thye

see 18 C5

Keep your meals saucy the Singaporean way with these moreish chilli and soya sauces. *10am-10pm*

Eu Yan Sang

see 18 C5

Founded in 1879, its curative supplements and tonics formulated under traditional Chinese medicine theory are trusted by all. *10am-10pm*

See p149
for eating and
drinking listings

Explore Northern & Central Singapore

Despite Singapore's reputation as a dense city of skyscrapers and high-rise living, swathes of wilderness can still be found in its north and central region. The 24km Rail Corridor trail slices through the island's central forests, with plenty of access points leading to hidden quarries, heritage bridges and even Singapore's highest peak.

This area blends natural wonders with nostalgic traces of a slower, rural past. Spend a day at Mandai Wildlife Reserve with its conglomeration of five wildlife parks, all dedicated to conservation education. Or go off the beaten track to find Singapore's last village, its only natural hot spring and other curiosities outside the downtown area.

Getting Around

MRT

This area of Singapore is encircled by the North–South Line and crisscrossed by the Downtown Line. Many of the nature reserves can be accessed on the Downtown Line.

Taxi

The most convenient way to explore the area; if cost is a consideration, couple your trip with an MRT ride.

Bus

Services are plenty; however, this area is vast so you'll spend a lot of time travelling to more-out-of-the-way sights.

Kebun Baru Birdsinging Club (p148)

MARCIAL GOMES/SHUTTERSTOCK

THE BEST

HIKING Rail Corridor (p144)

ZOO Mandai Wildlife Reserve (p142)

NATURE RESERVE MacRitchie Reservoir (p147)

WAR MUSEUM Former Ford Factory (p146)

HEARTLAND SPOT Kebun Baru Birdsinging Club (p148)

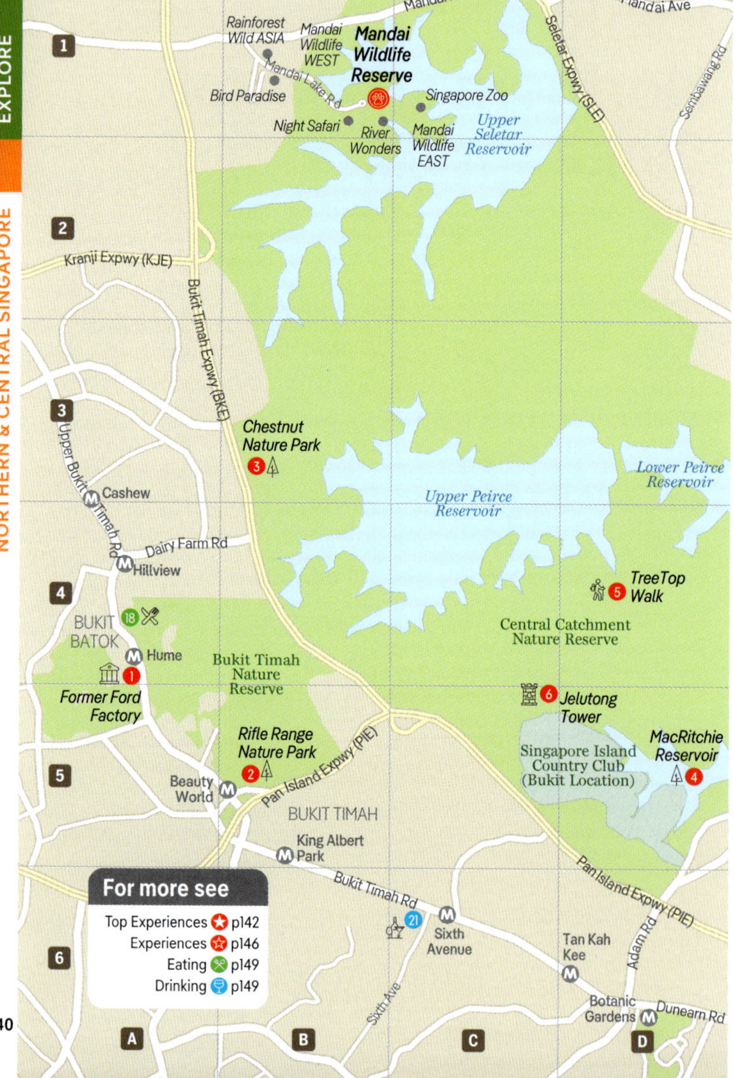
A
B
C
D
1
2
3
4
5
6
Mandai Rd
Mandai Ave
Rainforest Wild ASIA
Mandai Wildlife WEST
Mandai Wildlife Reserve
Mandai Lake Rd
Bird Paradise
Singapore Zoo
Night Safari
River Wonders
Mandai Wildlife EAST
Upper Seletar Reservoir
Seletar Expwy (SLE)
Sembawang Rd
Kranji Expwy (KJE)
Bukit Timah Expwy (BKE)
Chestnut Nature Park
Upper Bukit Timah Rd
Cashew
Lower Peirce Reservoir
Upper Peirce Reservoir
Dairy Farm Rd
Hillview
TreeTop Walk
BUKIT BATOK
Central Catchment Nature Reserve
Hume
Bukit Timah Nature Reserve
Former Ford Factory
Jelutong Tower
Rifle Range Nature Park
MacRitchie Reservoir
Singapore Island Country Club (Bukit Location)
Beauty World
Pan Island Expwy (PIE)
BUKIT TIMAH
King Albert Park
Bukit Timah Rd
Sixth Avenue
Tan Kah Kee
Adam Rd
Sixth Ave
Botanic Gardens
Dunearn Rd
For more see
Top Experiences p142
Experiences p146
Eating p149
Drinking p149

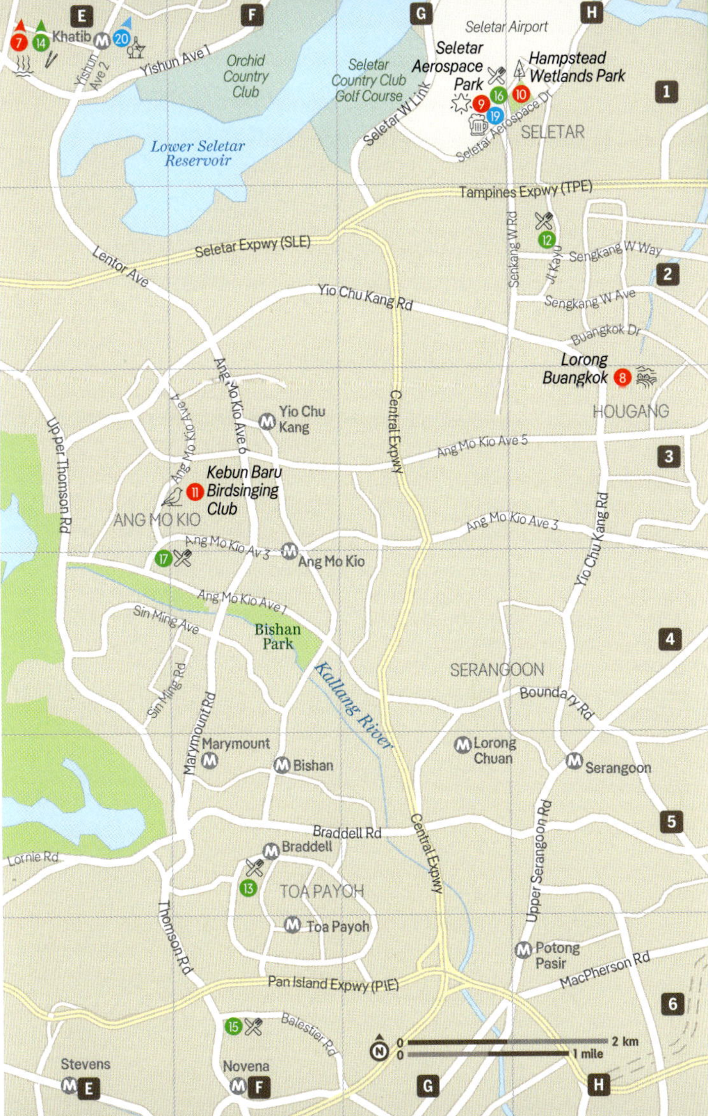
Khatib
Yishun Ave 1
Yishun Ave 2
Orchid Country Club
Lower Seletar Reservoir
Seletar Country Club Golf Course
Seletar Airport
Seletar Aerospace Park
Hampstead Wetlands Park
Seletar W Link
Seletar Aerospace Dr
SELETAR
Tampines Expwy (TPE)
Seletar Expwy (SLE)
Lentor Ave
Yio Chu Kang Rd
Senkang W Rd
Jl Kayu
Sengkang W Way
Sengkang W Ave
Buangkok Dr
Lorong Buangkok
HOUGANG
Ang Mo Kio Ave 6
Ang Mo Kio Ave 4
Yio Chu Kang
Central Expwy
Ang Mo Kio Ave 5
Upper Thomson Rd
Kebun Baru Birdsinging Club
ANG MO KIO
Ang Mo Kio Av 3
Ang Mo Kio
Ang Mo Kio Ave 3
Yio Chu Kang Rd
Ang Mo Kio Ave 1
Sin Ming Ave
Bishan Park
Kallang River
SERANGOON
Boundary Rd
Sin Ming Rd
Marymount Rd
Marymount
Bishan
Lorong Chuan
Serangoon
Braddell Rd
Braddell
Lornie Rd
TOA PAYOH
Central Expwy
Upper Serangoon Rd
Thomson Rd
Toa Payoh
Potong Pasir
MacPherson Rd
Pan Island Expwy (PIE)
Balestier Rd
Stevens
Novena
0 2 km
0 1 mile
E F G H
1 2 3 4 5 6
7 8 9 10 11 12 13 14 15 16 17 19 20

★ TOP EXPERIENCE

Mandai Wildlife Reserve

An unforgettable animal adventure awaits at Mandai Wildlife Reserve *(mandai.com)*, an integrated nature and wildlife precinct which has been lauded as one of the best reserves in the world for its conservation and educational efforts.

MAP P140 **B1**

PLANNING TIP
Save money with a Destination Pass which gives you a discount on visiting multiple parks. Pass validity ranges from one to 30 days.

Scan this QR code for opening hours, prices and tickets.

Mandai Wildlife EAST

Sprawled across 26 hectares, **Singapore Zoo** is a tropical wonderland with over 4200 animals in spacious natural enclosures and many roaming across wide open spaces. Enjoy barrier-free encounters with ring-tailed lemurs, lories and sloths at the giant Fragile Forest biodome. A highlight is Breakfast in the Wild, a morning buffet enjoyed in the company of wildlife ambassadors.

As darkness falls, you're transported into the heart of a jungle teeming with wildlife at **Night Safari**, the world's first nocturnal zoo. Open-sided electric shuttles guide visitors past nearly 130 species, including tigers and elephants; or explore on foot along atmospheric trails. Kids will delight in Creatures of the Night, a 20-minute interactive show featuring otters, raccoon dogs and bearded pigs.

The **River Wonders** wildlife park showcases the underwater realms of rivers around the world, like the Mekong River exhibit brimming with colossal catfish and stingrays, and the Amazon Flooded Forest, home to majestic manatees and gigantic arapaimas. The Giant Panda Forest draws crowds with rare red pandas and celebrity duo, KaiKai and JiaJia. Don't miss the Amazon River Quest Boat Ride, gliding past jaguars, tapirs and giant anteaters.

DANNY YE/SHUTTERSTOCK

Mandai Wildlife WEST

A sanctuary to more than 400 bird species, **Bird Paradise** is divided into eight walk-through aviaries that replicate habitats from across the world. Of note is the Ocean Network Express Penguin Cove, one of the world's biggest cold salt-water habitats. The Sky Amphitheatre features birds of prey at Predators on Wings, and pelicans and flamingos at Wings of the World.

Mandai's first wildlife adventure park, **Rainforest Wild ASIA** recreates iconic natural landscapes for adventure activities – novel experiences but the top-up charges for each activity add up quickly. Climb Karst mountains (pictured) at Wild Apex Adventure as curious François' langur monkeys judge you from adjacent rocks. Wild Cavern Adventure is a three-hour caving course through tight tunnels with just your headlamp; sessions start every hour.

QUICK BREAK

There are some food outlets in the parks, but most are located at the areas outside the entrances at Mandai Wildlife WEST and Mandai Wildlife EAST.

Walk the Rail Corridor

The Central Trail is the most compelling stretch of the historic Rail Corridor, the railway line that once crossed Singapore, connecting passengers and cargo to Malaysia. Dotted with old rail bridges and relics, this green corridor links key nature reserves and offers one of the island's most scenic walking routes.

START	END	LENGTH
Hume MRT Station	Bukit Timah Station	3.8km; 1hr

Dairy Farm Nature Park
0 500 m
0 0.25 miles
Upper Bukit Timah Truss Bridge
Hume Ave
START
Hume
Singapore Quarry Bridge
Bukit Timah Nature Reserve
Bukit Timah Expwy (BKE)
Bukit Batok Nature Reserve
Bukit Timah Nature Reserve Stone Marker
Old Jurong Rd
Upper Bukit Timah Rd
Rifle Range Rd
Hindhede Crossing
Colugo Deck
Rifle Range Nature Park
Cheong Chin Nam Rd
Jln Jurong Kechil
Beauty World
Toh Tuck Rd
Bukit Timah Truss Bridge
Dunearn Rd
Pan Island Expwy (PIE)
Clementi Rd
END

1 Historic Turning Point

Emerging from Hume MRT station (DT4), it's a five-minute walk south along Upper Bukit Timah Rd to the **Former Ford Factory** (p146) to learn about Singapore's WWII history and see the Surrender Room where the British capitulation to the Japanese took place.

2 Repurposed Quarters

Walk back up Upper Bukit Timah Rd for 15 minutes until you see the black beams of Upper Bukit Timah Truss Bridge. Cross the bridge to the **Rail Mall**, a row of single-storey shophouses with arches above their signs that were former workers' quarters for the rubber plantation once located here. This entrance to the Rail Corridor is marked by the old 9-Mile Platform.

3 Hidden Quarry Views

A five-minute walk southwards reveals the **Singapore Quarry Bridge** overhead. Take the staircase to the right, cross the bridge and join the paved road to the picturesque **Singapore Quarry** five minutes away; a former granite quarry turned into a picturesque lake for bird-watching.

4 More Picturesque Quarries

Double back to the Rail Corridor and keep walking south till **Hindhede Crossing**. Go down the stairs on the left and follow Hindhede Dr to the Bukit Timah Nature Reserve stone marker past the car park. A five-minute stroll on the boardwalk leads to the idyllic **Hindhede Quarry Lookout Point** overlooking another quarry lake.

5 Singapore's Highest Peak

If you're still raring to go, make the 1.2km climb up the Main Rd to **Bukit Timah Summit**, 163m high and snap a shot with the marker stone. Going north will connect you to Dairy Farm Nature Park for more forest trekking, but double back on the same route to return to the rail corridor.

6 Beauty World Break

Keep walking south until you hit the Beauty World Exit. Turn right and take a break at the **Beauty World Centre** shopping mall or the many small eateries along Cheong Chin Nam Rd. Turning right takes you to Rifle Range Nature Park (p146) and its scenic Colugo Deck viewpoint.

7 Restored Railway Relics

Another 15-minute walk south will take you to the **Bukit Timah Truss Bridge** crossing the major road below. A little further on is the **Bukit Timah Railway Station**, an unassuming brick building built in 1932 and carefully restored to become a mini heritage gallery.

EXPERIENCES

Learn about WWII at the Former Ford Factory

MUSEUM

MAP: 1 P140 A4

The former Ford Motors assembly plant is best remembered as the place where the British surrendered Singapore to the Japanese on 15 February 1942. It's now home to the **Former Ford Factory** *(corporate.nas.gov.sg; admission S$7.13)*, a museum that charts Singapore's descent into war, the three dark years of Japanese occupation, and Singapore's recovery and path to independence. This sombre story is told through audio interviews, newsreels and harrowing personal accounts. A highlight of the exhibition is the Surrender Room – the boardroom where the surrender took place. Learn more through free English guided tours on Saturday and Sunday at 11am and 3.30pm. Take the MRT to Hume station and walk five minutes down Upper Bukit Timah Rd. The museum is closed on Monday.

Hike Rifle Range Nature Park

NATURE PARK

MAP: 2 P140 B5

Established in 2022 as a buffer for Bukit Timah Nature Reserve, the 66-hectare **Rifle Range Nature Park** *(nparks.gov.sg)* occupies the site of the former Sin Seng Quarry. Learn about conservation at the Visitor Pavilion before traversing the elevated **Gliders Boardwalk** to the **Quarry Wetland**, a freshwater ecosystem backed by cliffs. Hike the **Colugo Trail** for a panorama of the quarry; choose between the 30m steep trail or the moderate 50m stepped route. Look out for animal-crossing features such as rope bridges and colugo poles along the way!

Go Mountain Biking at Chestnut Nature Park

NATURE PARK

MAP: 3 P140 B3

Mountain bikers, take note! **Chestnut Nature Park** *(nparks.gov.sg)* is the first park in Singapore with dedicated mountain-biking trails, from beginner to crazy advanced.

HISTORY OF THE RAIL CORRIDOR

The railway line that transported passengers and cargo between Singapore and the Malay peninsula for over 100 years was launched in 1903. It saw many tweaks, including the deviation of its original tracks for its southern leg, and a failed branch line to the western Jurong industrial area. The railway tracks and its surrounding lands were laid by the former Malayan Railway (Keretapi Tanah Melayu Berhad or KTM) and officially belonged to Malaysia. Only after the railway closed in 2011 were land parcels exchanged and Singapore started to develop the Rail Corridor as we know it today, a continuous green artery through the island.

Novices can practise in the two skill parks, while daredevils can execute drop-offs and jumps at the pump track. Set across 81 hectares of dense jungle, this is also Singapore's largest nature park, woven with hiking trails that run adjacent to the bike paths, separated by a barrier. Toilets, water fountains and bike rentals *(from S$15 per hr)* are available at Chestnut Point.

To get here, take the Bukit Panjang LRT to Pending LRT station, then walk 20 minutes southeast along Bukit Panjang Rd and Chestnut Ave.

Stroll above the Trees at MacRitchie Reservoir

NATURE RESERVE

Right in the centre of Singapore, **MacRitchie Reservoir** (MAP: 4 P140 **D5**; *nparks.gov.sg*) is a lush green space carved around the massive Central Catchment Area. The nature reserve has six trails ranging from 3km to 11km; the most popular is the 11km loop around the reservoir. This is one of the best places in Singapore for wildlife spotting, but the macaques can be aggressive – don't feed or antagonise them.

MacRitchie's biggest appeal is the **TreeTop Walk** (MAP: 5 P140 **D4**), a free-standing, 250m-long suspension bridge giving an aerial view of the forest canopy from 25m above the ground. A kilometre south, the thick foliage parts to unveil the **Jelutong Tower** (MAP: 6 P140 **C5**), an eight-storey panoramic structure with spiralling stairs and impressive canopy views.

Relax in Sembawang Hot Spring Park

HOT SPRING

MAP: 7 P140 **E1**

It comes as a surprise to many that a hot spring exists in Singapore, an island famously sheltered from tectonic activity. Discovered in 1909, the Sembawang hot spring became popular with locals, who believed the water was curative and therapeutic. What started as a tap in the ground is now the **Sembawang Hot Spring Park** *(nparks.gov.sg)*. At the cascading pool, water drawn up directly from the ground (at a sizzling 70°C) cools down naturally to 40°C in the lower tier where you can sit and soak your feet. Leave your swimsuit at home – you're only allowed to dip your feet in! A special feature is the egg station. Place your eggs in a small container and let the steaming hot-spring water work its magic. You will need to bring your own eggs, containers and cutlery.

Time-Travel at Heritage Village Lorong Buangkok

VILLAGE

MAP: 8 P140 **H3**

Singapore has developed so quickly that the island's once-ubiquitous *kampongs* (villages) have all but disappeared. Just one remains on the main island – the wonderfully rustic **Lorong Buangkok**. It offers an evocative experience of life in

Singapore before independence. The 26 remaining families who live here seem carefree and oblivious to the breakneck pace of life outside their rural oasis (the S$6 to S$30 monthly rent probably helps). The area is tiny, so 30 minutes to look around is plenty.

Enjoy Aviation-Themed Fun at Seletar Aerospace Park

LIFESTYLE DESTINATION

Seletar Aerospace Park (MAP: 9 P140 **G1**) is something of a local secret. During the colonial days, the British Royal Air Force station here served Singapore from 1928 to 1971. Today, the area is dominated by the tiny Seletar Airport and black-and-white houses transformed into an assembly of restaurants, spas and shops. The plane-inspired outdoor playground is perfect for the little ones.

Twitchers and aviation enthusiasts flock to the boardwalk near Hyde Park Gate for prime plane-spotting (mostly private jets) and to explore the nearby **Hampstead Wetlands Park** (MAP: 10 P140 **H1**), a marshland ideal for bird-watching.

Listen to History at Kebun Baru Birdsinging Club

LOCAL HANGOUT

MAP: 11 P140 **F3**

An unusual sight sits at the foot of Ang Mo Kio Town Garden West: a small field crowded with nearly 400 tall metal poles rising from the ground. This is the **Kebun Baru Birdsinging Club**, one of Singapore's last pockets of a once-widespread pastime. Visit on a weekend morning and you'll see colourful songbirds in ornate cages hoisted high atop the poles, while their proud owners gather below, chatting, comparing notes and listening closely to the chorus above. Regular singing competitions keep the tradition lively. For visitors, it's a rare window into old-school Singaporean life and local culture.

SINGAPORE'S REPURPOSED QUARRIES

The demand for public housing and roads in Singapore during the 1980s and '90s led to a spike in demand for granite, which was mined from several quarries in the hills around Bukit Timah and Bukit Batok. By 2000, encroaching residential areas and the dangers of quarry mining led to the quarries being shut down, filled in and transformed into picturesque neighbourhood parks teeming with wildlife. While most quarries are filled with water to form deep quarry pools, Dairy Farm Quarry at Dairy Farm Nature Park is unusual because it was filled in with earth instead.

See p140 for map of locations

Best Places for...

$ Budget $$ Midrange $$$ Top End

Eating

Local Eats & Treats

Jalan Kayu Thasevi Food $

12 H2

This place has been tossing up some of Singapore's best *roti prata* (Indian flatbread) and fish curry since the 1960s. *24hr*

Come Daily Fried Hokkien Prawn Mee $

13 F5

This noodle stall has a huge following, thanks to the crispy lard peppered throughout the noodles. *8.30am-2pm Wed-Sun*

Chong Pang Nasi Lemak $

14 E1

A household name serving nasi lemak, aromatic rice doused in spicy sambal and served with a crispy chicken wing. *5pm-6am*

Loong Fatt Tau Sar Piah $

15 F6

Popular for handmade *tau sar piah*, a gorgeously flaky and buttery Hokkien-style pastry filled with salty or sweet bean paste. *7.30am-4.30pm Mon-Sat*

Standout Dining

Wheeler's Estate $$$

16 G1

A favourite weekend destination comprising a restaurant and bar in a colonial-era building, and alfresco lawnside cafe with live music. *hours vary Tue-Sun*

Mellben Seafood $$

17 E4

Widely considered the best crabs in town. Signature dishes are clay-pot crab *bee hoon* (rice vermicelli noodles), butter crab and chilli crab. *5-11pm*

Acqua e Farina $$

18 A4

This cosy Italian restaurant at Rail Mall uses only the freshest ingredients for its dishes; the house-made pasta is a showstopper. *11.30am-2.30pm & 5.30-10pm Tue-Sun*

Drinking

Bars for a Night Out

Youngs Bar & Restaurant

19 G1

This black-and-white bungalow is the idyllic spot for a pint of Erdinger and modern European dishes. *11.30am-11pm Mon-Thu, to midnight Fri, 8am-midnight Sat, 10am-11pm Sun*

Nelson Bar

20 E1

Near the Sembawang Wharf, Nelson Bar has retained its history through sailors' old pictures and scribbles on its walls. *2pm-midnight*

Lazy Lizard

21 C6

Located just off busy Bukit Timah Rd, the outdoor patio fills with workers downing a few on their way home. *3pm-midnight Mon-Thu, 2pm-1am Fri, 2pm-2am Sat, 2pm-11pm Sun*

See p160
for eating,
drinking and
shopping
listings

Explore West & Southwest Singapore

Researched by Ria de Jong

Despite Singapore's image as a planned Garden City, pockets of wild terrain are still found in the west and southwest. This region hosts some of the country's finest nature reserves, offering underrated opportunities for hiking and wildlife enthusiasts.

Historically, the west remained less developed, a world apart from downtown urbanisation. The 1970s witnessed significant clearing of greenery for industry and residential expansion. Today, the western district is Singapore's primary manufacturing hub. While perhaps less renowned than downtown districts, it offers a nature-rich counterpoint for visitors with time to explore beyond the metropolitan core.

Getting Around

Singapore's west and southwest is a fairly large area. Not all sights are conveniently reached by public transport, so group them by location to minimise travel time.

MRT

This vast area is served fairly well by the MRT; lines currently under construction will add to the area's accessibility.

Taxi

For more out-of-the-way places, take a taxi from the MRT.

Bus

Extensive bus routes connect to MRT stations, but relying solely on them for your journey can be quite time-consuming.

Rhinoceros hornbill, Sungei Buloh Wetland Reserve (p155)
CHANSENCLICKS/SHUTTERSTOCK

THE BEST

HIKE Southern Ridges (p156)

WILDLIFE RESERVE Sungei Buloh Wetland Reserve (p155)

THEME PARK Haw Par Villa (p154)

WAR MUSEUM Reflections at Bukit Chandu (p157)

POTTERY STUDIO Thow Kwang Pottery Jungle (p159)

For more see
Top Experiences p154
Experiences p158
Eating p160
Drinking p161
Shopping p161

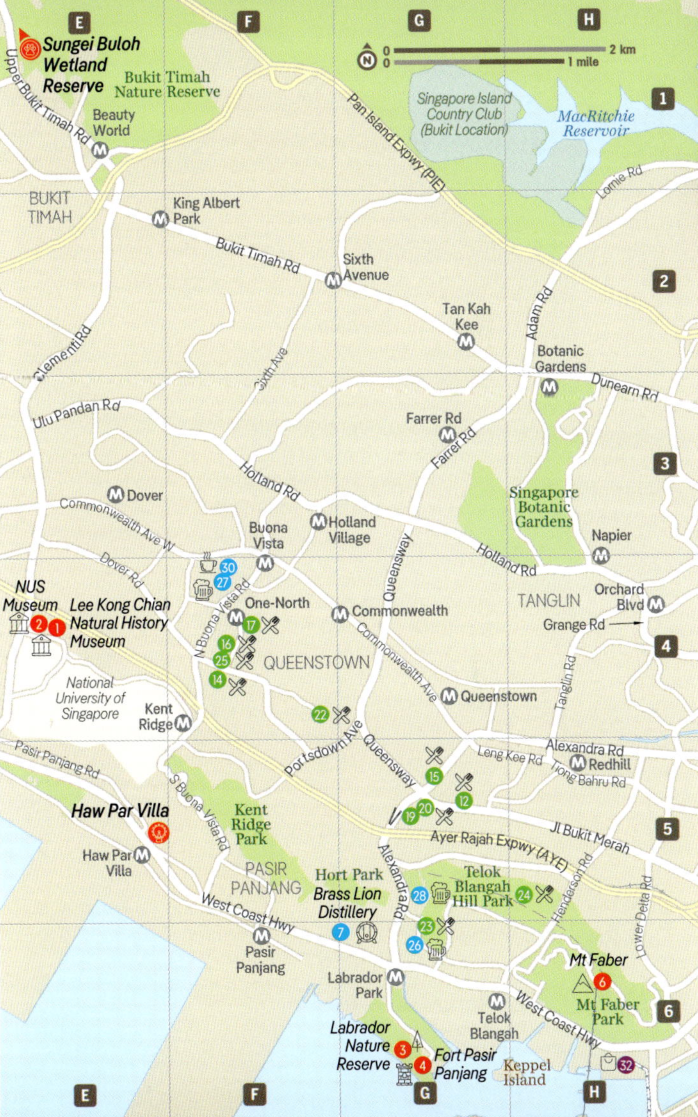
Sungei Buloh Wetland Reserve
Bukit Timah Nature Reserve
Beauty World
Upper Bukit Timah Rd
BUKIT TIMAH
King Albert Park
Bukit Timah Rd
Sixth Avenue
Pan Island Expwy (PIE)
Singapore Island Country Club (Bukit Location)
MacRitchie Reservoir
Lornie Rd
Tan Kah Kee
Adam Rd
Botanic Gardens
Dunearn Rd
Clementi Rd
Sixth Ave
Ulu Pandan Rd
Farrer Rd
Holland Rd
Dover
Commonwealth Ave W
Buona Vista
Holland Village
Queensway
Singapore Botanic Gardens
Napier
Dover Rd
NUS Museum
Lee Kong Chian Natural History Museum
N Buona Vista Rd
One-North
Commonwealth
TANGLIN
Orchard Blvd
Grange Rd
QUEENSTOWN
Commonwealth Ave
Tanglin Rd
National University of Singapore
Kent Ridge
Queenstown
Portsdown Ave
Leng Kee Rd
Alexandra Rd
Redhill
Tiong Bahru Rd
Pasir Panjang Rd
S Buona Vista Rd
Haw Par Villa
Kent Ridge Park
Ayer Rajah Expwy (AYE)
Jl Bukit Merah
Haw Par Villa
PASIR PANJANG
Hort Park
Brass Lion Distillery
Alexandra Rd
Telok Blangah Hill Park
Henderson Rd
Lower Delta Rd
West Coast Hwy
Pasir Panjang
Labrador Park
Mt Faber
Mt Faber Park
Telok Blangah
West Coast Hwy
Labrador Nature Reserve
Fort Pasir Panjang
Keppel Island
2 km
1 mile
EXPLORE
WEST & SOUTHWEST SINGAPORE

★ TOP EXPERIENCE

Haw Par Villa

Eccentric Haw Par Villa is the brainchild of Aw Boon Haw and Aw Boon Par, sons of the man behind the famous Tiger Balm. It reflects the family's passion for Chinese culture, depicting classic myths, legends and moral tales in fanciful dioramas.

MAP P152 **E5**

PLANNING TIP
Go early or late to avoid the midday heat and enjoy softer light for photos. Free online guides bring each quirky scene to life with hidden stories and local legends.

Mythical Mayhem

Haw Par Villa *(hawparvilla.sg)* hosts a riotous maze of dioramas: keep your eyes peeled for the Monkey King's wild antics from Journey to the West, the tragic romance of Madam White Snake and scenes from Chinese legends. Don't miss the giant Laughing Buddha, heroic generals astride tigers, and cheeky animal-human hybrids – each tableau is brimming with quirky details and storytelling magic.

Descend into Hell

Step into the dimly lit tunnel of the Ten Courts of Hell at the **Hell's Museum**, where each chilling tableau invites uneasy reflection on life's choices. Locals recall childhood visits that sparked equal parts fear and fascination. Wander slowly, letting each gruesome scene reveal its moral lesson. The horror is both cautionary and captivating, prompting visitors to weigh right and wrong long after leaving this surreal museum.

After-Dark Thrills

For a different kind of nightlife, join the **Journey to Hell** *(journeys.com.sg; adult/child S$40/20)* by Journeys Heritage Tours every Friday at 6.30pm. This two-hour walk through Haw Par Villa and the eerie Hell's Museum blends history, humour and ghost stories into a spine-tingling adventure – perfect for anyone craving something memorably macabre!

Scan the QR code for opening hours and museum tickets.

★ TOP EXPERIENCE

Sungei Buloh Wetland Reserve

Over half of Singapore's bird species find sanctuary alongside seasonal migratory visitors escaping the winter chill at Sungei Buloh Wetland Reserve. Covering more than 200 hectares of mudflats, mangroves, ponds and forests, this sprawling reserve offers an immersive escape into nature.

Walking Trails & Boardwalks

MAP P152 **E1**

The wetlands *(nparks.gov.sg/sbwr)* are bursting with life, so lace up your hiking shoes and begin your adventure at the **Coastal Trail**, offering sweeping views of the Straits of Johor. Duck into the lush greenery of the **Forest Trail**, where cool, dense canopies provide shade for you and a variety of wildlife – keep an eye out for butterflies, birds and monitor lizards. Finally, meander along the **Mangrove Boardwalk** to marvel at twisted roots and bustling mudflats. Stay alert as you might spot darting mudskippers, smooth-coated otters or even a stealthy crocodile.

PLANNING TIP
Early morning or early evening are the best times to visit, especially during low tide, and binoculars make the experience even better. The migratory bird season runs from September to March.

Mangrove Gallery & Nature Gallery

Learn about mangroves and the creatures that call the mud home at the Visitor Centre's **Mangrove Gallery**. Then visit the Wetland Centre's **Nature Gallery** to discover local wildlife and their habitats. Take your time with the interactive exhibits and enjoy a hands-on learning experience.

Buloh Tidal Ponds

Walk around this carefully restored freshwater habitat, teeming with diverse plants and wildlife. Visit at low tide for the best views, and use the camouflaged bird-watching huts and tower to quietly observe migratory birds in their natural surroundings.

Scan this QR Code for park opening hours, directions and updates.

WALKING TOUR

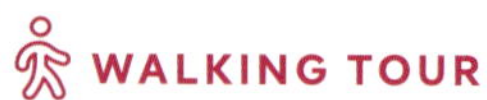

Hike the Southern Ridges

Made up of a series of parks and hills, the Southern Ridges will have you trekking through the jungle without ever really leaving the city. The best stretch is from Kent Ridge Park to Mt Faber. It's relatively easy and offers forest-canopy walkways, lofty skyline vistas and the spectacular Henderson Waves.

START	END	LENGTH
Kent Ridge Park	Mt Faber Park	6.6km; 2½hr

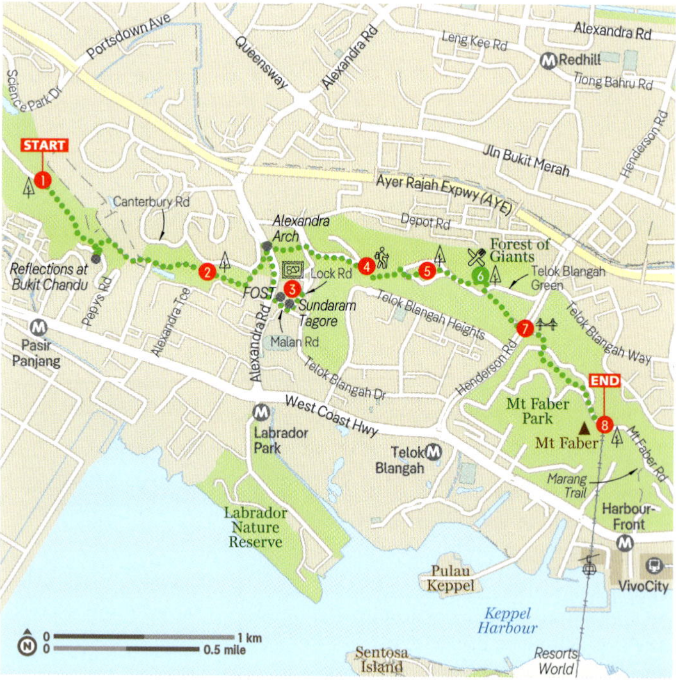

1 A Poignant War Museum

Start at peaceful **Kent Ridge Park**, where an elevated canopy will take you through a treetop boardwalk to **Reflections at Bukit Chandu**. This small but powerful WWII museum tells the story of the Malay Regiment in the Battle of Pasir Panjang (p159), when the Japanese invaded in 1942.

2 Get Lost in Gardens

Next, journey down the hill to **Hort-Park**, where you'll discover five distinct zones teeming with themed gardens as well as playgrounds, dining options and innovative glass-houses that served as prototypes for the renowned cooled conservatories at Gardens by the Bay.

3 A Creative Detour

Depart HortPark via Alexandra Rd, heading south and turning left into Malan Rd and again into Lock Rd for rambling leisure outpost **Gill-man Barracks**. Built in 1936 as a British military encampment, it is now home to contemporary art galleries, funky cafes and trendy restaurants. Notable stops include **Sundaram Tagore Gallery**, showcasing names like Edward Burtynsky and Annie Leibovitz, and **FOST Gallery**, championing Singapore's emerging talent.

4 Take to the Trees

Retrace your steps along Alexandra Rd and venture across **Alexandra Arch**, an 80m-long bridge that resembles a leaf unfurling above the road. Proceed along the **Forest Walk**, an elevated walkway lead-ing through the forest canopy that has drawn over 200 bird species to the hillside.

5 A Colour-Popping Garden

You've reached **Telok Blangah Hill Park**, best known for its picturesque Terrace Garden. Here, bougainvilleas add a bright pop of colour to the semicircular terraces that offer a 360-degree vista of Singapore.

6 A Hillside Nosh Spot

Feeling peckish? Grab a bite at **Wildseed Cafe** at the stunningly restored colonial-era bungalow **Alkaff Mansion**. Fuelled up, continue on to admire the rare towering trees at the Forest of Giants.

7 Walk the Wave

From here, it's a short walk to one of the Southern Ridges' high-lights across Henderson Rd: the undulating sculptural wonder of the 36m-high **Henderson Waves**, the tallest pedestrian bridge in Singapore.

8 A Peak View

On the other side of the bridge is **Mt Faber Park**, one of the island's oldest parks, with panoramic views of the southern coastline from its peak, **Mt Faber** (p158). From here, you can go downhill via the Marang Trail, by taxi or the most exciting option – cable car.

EXPERIENCES

Go Back to School at the National University of Singapore

MUSEUMS

The National University of Singapore campus is home to two underrated museums. The grassy, boulder-like building that houses the **Lee Kong Chian Natural History Museum** (MAP: 1 P152 **E4**; *lkcnhm.nus.edu.sg; adult/child S$24/15*) displays over a million specimens showcasing the biodiversity of Southeast Asia and Singapore, and has a historical collection dating back to the 19th century. It's a high-tech, family-friendly museum with lots of interactive elements.

Next door, the **NUS Museum** (MAP: 2 P152 **E4**; *museum.nus.edu.sg; free*) collection has more than 8000 artworks and artefacts ranging from ancient Chinese ceramics and classical Indian sculptures to contemporary Southeast Asian art pieces. Don't miss the works of celebrated Singaporean sculptor Ng Eng Teng, the 'Grandfather of Singapore sculpture'.

Uncover the Secrets of Labrador Nature Reserve

NATURE RESERVE

The smallest of Singapore's nature reserves at just 10 hectares, **Labrador Nature Reserve** (MAP: 3 P152 **G6**; *nparks.gov.sg*) offers its visitors more than a quick walk. Wildlife lovers will appreciate Singapore's only rocky sea cliff that can be found on the mainland and the three boardwalks that meander through mangroves and forests. History buffs can explore the artillery remains of **Fort Pasir Panjang** (MAP: 4 P152 **G6**), which once defended nearby Keppel Harbour.

Learn & Play at the Science Centre Singapore

MUSEUM

The **Science Centre Singapore** (MAP: 5 P152 **B2**; *science.edu.sg; adult/child S$12/8*) is fun no matter how old you are. It's home to more than 20 interactive galleries that explore varied topics such as ecosystems, human anatomy and optical illusions, with regular shows and demonstrations. Its **Omni-Theatre** *(S$14)* has a giant IMAX screen, while sub-zero **Snow City** *(snowcity.com.sg; adult/child S$31/24)* with its snowy slope is perfect for escaping the heat. **KidsSTOP** *(adult/child peak S$13/23)* is a dedicated section for under-8s.

Ride the Cable Car to Mt Faber

CABLE CAR

MAP: 6 P152 **H6**

Formerly a signal hill and defence fort, **Mt Faber** *(nparks.gov.sg)* is one of the best spots for sweeping views of Singapore's southern coastline. The peak marks one end of the Southern Ridges walk (p156), but most visitors come for the cable car (*mountfaberleisure.com; adult/child from S$35/25*) linking HarbourFront and Sentosa Island. For an extra thrill, hop into a SkyOrb

Cabin, the world's first chrome-finished spherical cable-car cabin with transparent glass floors.

Taste Gin at Brass Lion Distillery

DISTILLERY

MAP: 7 P152 **G6**

If you're curious about what a made-in-Singapore gin tastes like, visit the **Brass Lion Distillery** (*brassliondistillery.com; tours S$49, tastings S$70*), one of the island's gin pioneers. Tour the intimate distillery and its gleaming copper still, Nala. The signature Singapore Dry Gin blends 22 locally sourced botanicals, including lemongrass, torch ginger and galangal. Discover craft-gin secrets, stroll the on-site botanical garden, sample a flight of gins, then linger for cocktails and canapés in the Tasting Room.

Let Loose at Jurong Lake Gardens

GARDENS

Set aside a few hours to discover **Jurong Lake Gardens** (MAP: 8 P152 **B2**; *juronglakegardens.nparks.gov.sg*), Singapore's newest national garden, nestled in the heartlands and easily accessible via the Chinese Garden and Lakeside MRT stations. The expansive lakeside garden features winding boardwalks, kids' play areas and carefully preserved natural habitats. Photography enthusiasts should not miss the picture-perfect **Chinese Garden** (MAP: 9 P152 **B1**) and **Japanese Garden** (MAP: 10 P152 **B2**), celebrating Singapore's rich cultural heritage.

Potter Through Thow Kwang Pottery Jungle

POTTERY STUDIO

MAP: 11 P152 **A1**

Rooms at **Thow Kwang Pottery Jungle** (*potteryjungle.com; workshops from S$50*) overflow with teetering stacks of colourful ceramics, creating an irresistible maze for pottery lovers. It's home to Singapore's last surviving dragon kiln, still run by the Tan family, who've crafted ceramics here since 1965. Firing this wood-burning kiln is intense, so it only roars to life a few times a year, but hands-on pottery workshops run year-round. Few leave empty-handed.

THE BATTLE OF OPIUM HILL

Opium Hill (Bukit Chandu in Malay) stands on Pasir Panjang Ridge (now Kent Ridge) and was named after the opium-processing factory once located at its foot. The Battle of Pasir Panjang unfolded on 13 February 1942 during the defence of Singapore in WWII. Japanese forces sought to breach the Allied defences along the island's west coast. The Malay Regiment, made up primarily of local soldiers, heroically defended the ridge but the Japanese prevailed. The battle marked a crucial stage in the fall of Singapore, highlighting the determination of Allied forces and their ultimate defeat.

LISTINGS

Best Places for...

See p152 for map of locations

$ Budget $$ Midrange $$$ Top End

Eating

Hawker Bites

ABC Brickworks Food Centre $

12 G5

Fuel up here before or after hiking the Southern Ridges trail. *8am-11pm*

Clementi 448 Food Centre $

13 D3

Find all your beloved hawker favourites here. Arrive early or expect long queues. *7am-9pm*

Timbre+ One North $

14 F4

New-gen hawker centre with food trucks, street art, craft beer and live music (Monday to Saturday evenings). *7am-midnight Mon-Thu, to 1am Fri & Sat, 11am-10pm Sun*

Casual Eating Spots

CommonMan Coffee Roasters $$

15 G5

Known for epic all-day breakfasts. Try the flavourful Turkish Breakfast with a filo-wrapped soft-boiled egg complemented with feta, herbs, honey and pomegranate. *7.30am-5pm & 6-10pm Wed-Sun, 7.30am-5pm Mon & Tue*

One Fattened Calf Burgers $$

16 F4

Touted as one of the best burger joints; the fluffy potato buns have a cult following. The Combo chunky fries and golden lime slushie make the meal. *11am-3pm & 5-8pm Mon-Sat*

Jimmy Monkey Café $$

17 F4

Get a taste of Melbourne cafe culture at this funky little spot, known for its all-day brunch options and popular coffee blends. *8am-4pm*

Coexist Coffee Co. $$

18 D1

Perched on the top floor of an industrial building, this hidden cafe serves up hearty brunches and tasty lunches. *9am-6pm*

Cult Classics

Keng Eng Kee (KEK) Seafood $

19 G5

This family-run restaurant serves up hearty Chinese *zi char* (family-style sharing) dishes in a casual setting. *11.30am-2pm & 5-10pm*

Depot Road Zhen Shan Mei Claypot Laksa $

20 G5

There's always a queue for this stall's much-lauded bowls of laksa. *9am-3.30pm Mon, Tue & Thu-Sat*

Laifabai $$

21 D2

Cult-favourite *wonton mee* and wood-fired meats joint tucked away in Bukit Batok. *11.30am-3pm & 6-9pm Tue-Fri, 11am-3pm & 5.30-9pm Sat & Sun*

Fine Dining

Ce Soir $$$

22 F4

Flowers, fantasy and fine dining come together at this French restaurant housed in a black-and-white bungalow. 6.30-11pm Wed, *noon-3.30pm & 6.30-11pm Thu-Sun*

Naked Finn $$$

23 G6

Natural flavours with minimal seasoning shine through at this contemporary seafood restaurant. *noon-2.30pm & 6-9.30pm Mon-Sat*

Una $$$

 H5

Spanish powerhouse located in the Alkaff Mansion, the perfect backdrop for a romantic meal. *noon-2.30pm & 6-10.30pm Tue-Fri, 6-10.30pm Sat & Sun*

Casa Pietrasanta $$

 F4

Indulge in freshly made pasta and authentic dishes at this modern Italian joint. *11.30am-2.30pm & 5.30-10pm Mon-Sat*

Drinking

Beer Brews

Little Island Brewing Co @ Gillman Barracks

26 G6

Perfecting its brews on the island for nearly a decade. Enjoy your suds with moreish fermented-kombucha-dough charcoal pizzas. *noon-11pm Tue-Sat, to 10pm Sun*

Picotin Brewhaus

27 F4

Using traditional German brewing techniques and state-of-the-art cooling systems to ensure fresh and perfectly chilled brews. *11am-11pm*

Handlebar

 G5

As the sun dips motorcycles rumble into this biker-themed bar for ice-cold beers. *4-11pm Mon, noon-midnight Tue-Fri, 10am-1am Sat, 10am-11pm Sun*

Caffeine Hot Spots

Suzuki Gourmet Coffee

 A2

At Singapore's oldest coffee roaster, master baristas meticulously prepare each drop to awaken your senses. *8.30am-5.30pm Tue-Sun*

Dewgather

 F4

This Australian-inspired coffee spot uses sustainably sourced beans from South America to create an exclusive blend roasted in-house. *8am-10pm Mon-Sat, from 7.30am Sun*

Glass Roasters

 D3

This minimalist coffee stop seats only eight and offers a rotating selection of beans for an ever-evolving, impeccably crafted cup of coffee. *9am-5pm Wed-Mon*

Shopping

Mega Malls

VivoCity

 H6

Singapore's largest shopping centre has over 300 stores, mainly targeted at the midrange segment. It has waterfront dining options and a kids' playground. *10am-10pm*

Westgate

 C2

Family-friendly Westgate ticks all the boxes. Children will delight in Westgate Wonderland, an adventure playground with wet areas and a tree house. *10am-10pm*

IMM

34 C2

Offering over 90 outlet stores and touting discounts of up to 80% off retail prices, this is the place to hit if you're after a bargain. *10am-10pm*

See p172
for eating, drinking and shopping listings

Explore Sentosa Island

Researched by Morgan Awyong

Queuing for a ride at Universal Studios, it's hard to imagine that the resort island of Sentosa was once quiet, tree-filled Pulau Blakang Mati, home to an assortment of small fishing villages.

It became a defence outpost for the British in 1878, but in the 1970s, the island was renamed Sentosa and became a resort with a rotating slew of attractions. The place only really started to shine after Resorts World Sentosa came along in 2010, and at its peak, drew more than 19 million visitors a year.

Today Sentosa is manicured and acts as Singapore's playground for escapism, blending entertainment, luxury residences and tropical attractions in a 500-hectare haven.

Getting Around

Cable Car

Reach the island from Mt Faber or the HarbourFront Centre. A separate line then takes you deeper into the island with stops at Sensoryscape, Imbiah Lookout and Siloso Point.

Monorail

The Sentosa Express running from VivoCity links to the island's main attractions via three stops: Resorts World, Imbiah and Beach.

Bus

The 'beach tram' (an electric bus) shuttles the length of Sentosa's three beaches. Two standard bus sevices (A and B) link the main attractions and both depart from the bus stop beside Beach monorail station.

THE BEST

AQUARIUM Singapore Oceanarium (p165)

AMUSEMENT PARK Universal Studios (p166)

BEACH Palawan Beach (p170)

BEACH CLUB Tanjong Beach Club (p170)

WAR FORT Fort Siloso (p168)

Palawan Beach (p170)
SANGA PARK/SHUTTERSTOCK

Keppel Harbour
Adventure Cove Waterpark
Singapore Oceanarium
Causeway Bridge
Sentosa Gateway
Pulau Brani
For more see
Top Experiences p165
Experiences p170
Eating p172
Drinking p173
Shopping p173
Siloso Rd
Mt Imbiah
Imbiah Walk
Resorts World
Selat Sengkir
Mega Adventure
Waterfront
Universal Studios
Gateway Ave
Skypark Sentosa by AJ Hackett
Imbiah Rd
Imbiah
Loui's NY Pizza Parlor
Siloso Beach
Sensoryscape
Beach View Rd
Artillery Ave
Serapong Golf Course
Beach
See Enlargement
The Knolls
Mt Serapong
HyperDrive
Twelve
SENTOSA COVE
Ocean Dr
Palawan Island
Palawan Beach
Allanbrooke Rd
Bukit Manis Rd
Cove Dr
0 100 m
Skyline Luge
AltitudeX
Siloso Beach
Tanjong Golf Course
Wings of Time
Beach
Tanjong Beach Club
Tanjong Beach
0 500 m
0 0.25 miles
A B C D E F
1 2 3 4

★ TOP EXPERIENCE

Singapore Oceanarium

The Singapore Oceanarium has 22 zones that combine themed habitats with interactive elements and multimedia storytelling – an engaging and eye-opening adventure for all ages.

MAP P164 **C1**

Photogenic Depths

The showstopper comes immediately with **Ocean Wonders**. Featuring one of the world's largest sea-jelly habitats, your viral social-media moment awaits before the staggering 6.8m-diameter kreisel tank filled with countless drifting moon jellies. Equally dramatic is the **Whale Fall** room. Replicating a gigantic whale carcass on the seabed complete with a walkable rib-cage 'tunnel', it includes rare glimpses of the secretive creatures that live there. Most mesmerising is the **Trenches** hall, with ghostly deep-sea specimens frozen in midair – courtesy of a clear preservative.

PLANNING TIP
The attraction is massive so set aside at least two hours to take it all in. There are snack kiosks and a cafe inside for when you're peckish.

Take Your Time

Filled with tunnels and dwarf-sized viewing rooms for kids, the oceanarium *(singaporeoceanarium.com)* invites slow exploration with multiple seated zones for you to rest your feet. Apart from the occasional snack kiosk, there's also a full-fledged **Explorer's Nook** cafe at the **Spirit of Exploration** room for when you're hungry.

Integrated Learning

It isn't pure gawking either: there's a healthy sprinkle of education mixed in. Windows showcase staff at work in their labs, and touch pools at **Singapore's Coast** feature a chatty crew who dispense instruction and trivia as guests handle small sea critters. Deepen your experience by adding one of the special programmes while booking which include encounters with manta rays.

Scan this QR code for opening hours and to book ahead, including special packages.

★ TOP EXPERIENCE

Universal Studios

Southeast Asia's first and only Universal Studios is one of Universal's smaller parks but offers an array of thrilling rides and interactive shows alongside a slew of restaurants and shops, all themed after popular Hollywood blockbusters. There's something for everyone, from kid-friendly attractions to adrenaline-pumping rides.

MAP P164 **C2**

PLANNING TIP
If queuing up isn't your thing, it might be worth investing in a Universal Express pass (additional S$100), which lets you jump in the fast lane once for each participating ride.

Scan this QR code for opening hours and to book ahead.

Thrilling Roller-Coasters & Rides

For an adrenaline rush like no other, head straight to **Battlestar Galactica: HUMAN vs CYLON** – the world's tallest duelling roller-coaster. Opt for the red HUMAN track for an exciting ride, or amplify the thrills on the blue CYLON track, where your legs dangle freely. **Revenge of the Mummy** is a bumpy but exhilarating ride in search of the Book of the Living, while **TRANSFORMERS The Ride** uses 3D glasses to immerse you in the action as you zip through the city with the Autobots to fight the Decepticons. The **Jurassic Park Rapids Adventure** – closed at the time of writing – starts off as a leisurely float down a river that rapidly turns into something more exhilarating when the dinosaurs go on a rampage!

For the Kids

Good news for the faint-hearted or those with kids: not all the rides are gut-wrenchers. For milder thrills, Far Far Away is a good section to start in, with the junior roller-coasters **Puss in Boots: Giant Journey** and **Enchanted Airways**. Venture into Ancient Egypt for the popular **Treasure Hunters** ride, offering a unique 'drive' through an excavation site. To journey through space, hop aboard the **Sesame Street Spaghetti Space**

CHUA KOK BENG MARCUS/SHUTTERSTOCK

Chase, where Elmo and Grover guide you on an interstellar adventure fit for the whole family. The **Canopy Flyer** allows you to fly above the crowds like a pterodactyl, while **Dino-Soarin'** lets the kids go up, up and away astride their favourite flying dinosaur. At Minionland, the **Despicable Me Minion Mayhem** is a sensory riot as you transform into a Minion.

PIT STOP
Refuel with a pizza slice or pasta at **Loui's NY Pizza Parlor**. Those needing to feed a tribe can opt for a whole pizza (S$50).

Lights, Camera, Action!

Give your feet a well-deserved rest and enter the air-conditioned comfort of indoor entertainment. **Lights, Camera, Action! Hosted by Steven Spielberg** is a fun insight into movie magic and the wonders of special effects. Journey into the world of Shrek with the immersive **Shrek 4-D Adventure**. And don't miss the lively **Trolls: Hug Time Jubilee**, an all-singing, all-dancing spectacular.

WALKING TOUR

Walk Fort Siloso

Singapore's best-preserved coastal fort is on Sentosa Island. Built in the late 19th century by the British as a naval defence, Fort Siloso turned its guns inland during WWII after an unexpected invasion by the Japanese from Malaysia. The compound pays homage to this infamous chapter of Singapore's history.

START	END	LENGTH
Fort Siloso Skywalk	Fort Siloso Skywalk	1.3km; 1½hr

1 A Soaring Viewpoint

Bus A and the Beach Tram will drop you off at the Siloso Point stop. Cross the road, pick up a brochure, and take the lift up the 11-storey-tall **Siloso Skywalk**. The views are some of the best on the island, but sunglasses and umbrellas might help with the harsh sun.

2 A Military Orientation

At the end of the Skywalk, you'll face a 25-pounder howitzer gun made in 1939. This one's decommissioned but others are still used for gun salutes at national events. At this introduction area is also a small tunnel complex and the **Battery Command Post**.

3 Reliving WWII

Head down the stairs to the left of the command post to **Fort Siloso Square**. Here, a modest gallery chronicles the fall of Singapore with some prisoner-of-war (POW) art on display. After re-emerging at the square, admire the three cannon guns before walking down the gentle slope northwest.

4 Reaching Siloso Point

Pop into the Tunnel B Complex where ammunition was once stored, or continue on to reach the Engine Room and Store buildings. The road splits up here but carry on straight past the Wartime Staple Garden (using the Tunnel A Complex if you wish for a more eerie experience) to reach a tucked-away gem – the **Fire Director Tower**. This is the westernmost tip of the island, used to spot naval activity, and a room with wax figures and radio equipment recreates the scene.

5 An Era Ended

Double back to the Store buildings and this time, take the left fork past some small cannons and mortars to the **Surrender Chambers**. The presentation shows the pivotal moments leading up to the surrender of the British (and later the Japanese), with historical documents and audio clips. The two life-sized waxed-figure recreations of the historical handovers are especially poignant.

6 A Soldier's Life

Head east after you exit, and when you reach a granite brick wall, look for the hairpin path back to a guardroom. This begins a walk through a cluster of small buildings mimicking the military routines of the soliders based here. Besides the quarters and mess, there is also a parbuckling model illustrating how the heavy artillery was moved up the slopes. You'll complete the route after the **Quartermaster's Bungalow** and return to the Skywalk.

EXPERIENCES

Lounge on or Beside Sentosa's White-Sand Beaches BEACH CLUBS

If you'd prefer to skip the salty splashes and sandy toes, then take a dip in the crystal-clear pools of any beach club scattered along the coast of Sentosa. **Tanjong Beach Club** (MAP: 1 P164 D4; *tanjongbeachclub.com*) is a longstanding institution where chic coral-coloured sunshades and day beds are perfectly calculated to complement the turquoise waters. The music playlist is impeccable with coastal-forward beats.

For elevated views, head to **+Twelve** (MAP: 2 P164 C3; *thepalawansentosa.com/plustwelve*) in the Palawan lifestyle precinct. The adults-only club has a terraced structure with 12 private cabanas – each with its own plunge pool – that guarantees unblocked views. The vibes are amped up by the musical programme curated by the DJ Dispensary, shuttling between deep house and tropical beats to EDM and R&B. There's also a swim-up bar (the only beach club to have one) for an idyllic soak, and picnic tables are set out on **Palawan Beach** (MAP: 3 P164 C3) for those who love the crunch of sand beneath them.

Get Your Heart Pumping ADVENTURE SPORTS

If Universal Studios' roller-coasters and rides aren't exciting enough, Sentosa has plenty of other ways to satisfy adrenaline junkies. **Mega Adventure** (MAP: 4 P164 A2; *sg.megaadventure.com; from S$18*) has a climbing course and trampolines, but the highlight is **MegaZip**, the 450m-long zip line over the treetops and beach. At nearby **Skypark Sentosa by AJ Hackett** (MAP: 5 P164 A2; *skyparksentosa.com; from S$59*), challenge yourself with a 47m-high bungee jump or ride the giant swing over the sands of Siloso Beach. At **Skyline Luge** (MAP: 6 P164 B4; *sentosa.skylineluge.com; from S$31*), take the Skyride chairlift to the top of Mt Imbiah and then hurtle your luge down four winding sloped

THE COST OF ENTERING SENTOSA

Sentosa's admission fee depends on how you enter the island. Walking or cycling across the Sentosa Boardwalk bridge from the HarbourFront is completely free. Taking public bus 123 only requires the standard distance-based bus fare, while the Sentosa Express monorail from VivoCity costs $4 per person. If you're in a small group, consider taking a taxi, as this adds only $2 to $6 per vehicle to the base travel fare. The most scenic way to reach Sentosa is via cable car from Mt Faber or the HarbourFront Centre. Return tickets start from $32.90 and can go up to $47.40 depending on the cabin type.

tracks. After you're done, it's just a short walk to **AltitudeX** (MAP: 7 P164 B4; *altitudex.com; from S$79*), where you can free fall in one of the world's largest indoor wind tunnels (as high as six storeys). Racing enthusiasts will go nuts for Asia's first indoor gamified electric go-kart arena **HyperDrive** (MAP: 8 P164 B3; *thepalawansentosa.com/hyperdrive; from S$45*), where real-life racing and virtual gaming come together around a three-level indoor racetrack.

Splish, Splash & Snorkel at Adventure Cove Waterpark

WATERPARK

MAP: 9 P164 B1

Stay cool in Singapore's sultry humidity and have a splashing good time. **Adventure Cove Waterpark** (*rwsentosa.com; adult/child S$34/29*) has several twisting, spiralling water slides for thrill-seekers – the **Pipeline Plunge** is particularly exhilarating because you slide in the dark, but the bravest can attempt the **Riptide Rocket** for the steepest dips, made extra gravity-defying with the region's first hydro-magnetic coaster. Little ones can enjoy the kid-friendly **Big Bucket Treehouse** and **Seahorse Hideaway** water playgrounds. Those who prefer something more sedate can bob about in the giant wave pool at **Bluwater Bay** (weekends are great for a spot of DJ-led music), float the park along the **Adventure River** passing jungle flora and mysterious grotto caves, or head to **Rainbow Reef** for some snorkelling with more than 20,000 tropical fish – perfect for beginners with a phobia of open waters.

Stir Your Senses

GARDENS

Stretching between Imbiah Station and Beach Station, the six sculptural installations of **Sensoryscape** (MAP: 10 P164 B2; *sensoryscape.sentosa.com.sg; free*) make completing the 350m-long walkway feel that much shorter. Decked in lights and set on two levels, the pavilion-like structures each offer a different sensorial escape. Start with the **Lookout Loop** at Imbiah Station for a scenic overview of what's to come, and download the ImaginNite mobile app to reveal each stop's VR overlay. As you meander south through each point, follow the app's instructions to reveal cinematic effects from fluttering clouds of butterflies to marine animals drifting in space. **Tactile Trellis** has plants with textured surfaces to touch, while **Scented Sphere** focuses on naturally fragrant herbs and flowers to perfume the space. Come during the night to see them at their most magnificent, especially when nearby fireworks show **Wings of Time** (MAP: 11 P164 B4; *mountfaberleisure.com; seats from S$14*) sets off their nightly display.

LISTINGS

Best Places for...

$ Budget $$ Midrange $$$ Top End

See p164 for map of locations

Eating

Waterside Bites

Coastes $$
12 A3
Come for weekend breakfast and relaxed seaside vibes, or feast on pasta and pizza with frozen margaritas after a session of water sports. *hours vary*

Mykonos on the Bay $$
13 F3
Dine alfresco at this marina-flanking Greek taverna and tuck into Hellenic flavours that could make your *papou* weep. *noon-3pm & 6-10.30pm Mon-Wed & Fri, 6-10.30pm Thu, noon-10.30pm Sat & Sun*

FOC by the Beach $$$
14 C3
Tuck into some seriously moreish tapas, seafood and perfectly cooked paellas at this tiny slice of the Mediterranean on Palawan Beach. *11.30am-10.30pm Wed, Thu & Sun, to 11pm Fri & Sat*

Worth the Splurge

Ocean Restaurant $$$
15 B1
Savour modern European seafood as you watch manta rays, reef sharks and tropical fish glide past at this one-of-a-kind aquarium experience. *11.30am-3pm & 6-10.30pm Tue-Sun*

Cassia $$$
16 C3
Indulge in scrumptious Cantonese dim sum (lunchtime) or succulent seafood with a modern twist in the sophisticated ambience of Capella hotel. *noon-2.30pm & 6-10pm*

Empire Grill $$$
17 C3
Retreat into the sanctuary of Raffles Sentosa and tuck into the heavily seasonal wood-fire cuisine boasting Tuscan flavours. *12.30-10pm*

Cheaper Eats

Malaysian Food Street $
18 C1
This indoor hawker centre beside Universal Studios dishes up affordable street-food favourites from Singapore's neighbour. *8.30am-8.30pm*

Good Old Days Food Court $
19 B4
Near Beach Station, this food court offers Asian dishes, and the local offerings on the 2nd level are halal-certified. *hours vary*

International Food Street $
20 B4
A colourful beachside enclave of Kombi vans, food trucks and containers selling lip-smacking international street food at the Central Beach Bazaar. *11am-9pm*

Drinking

Best Beach Clubs

Tanjong Beach Club

see 1 D4

Coffee or cocktails, these snazzy beach daybeds are some of the best on the island filled with the glam set. *11am-10pm Mon-Fri, from 9am Sat & Sun*

Tipsy Unicorn Beach Club

21 A2

Looking like a set from the *Barbie* movie, this venue is cheeky fun with nighttime neon lights. *noon-10pm Tue-Thu & Sun, to midnight Fri & Sat*

Rumours Beach Club

22 A2

Sink into a plush sofa or daybed, immersing yourself in the laid-back ambience. Savour the panoramic views, three pools and handcrafted cocktails. *10am-10pm Fri-Sun, from 11am Mon-Thu*

+Twelve

see 2 C3

The only beach club on the island to have a swim-up bar and terraced private cabanas with attached pools. *11am-9pm Mon-Thu, 9.30am-10.30pm Fri-Sun*

Tipples with a View

1-Altitude Coast

23 B2

The infinity pool might be a little small but the attitude's big at the tallest bar on the island, perched atop sexy Outpost Hotel. *11am-10pm Mon & Tue, to 2am Fri & Sat, to midnight Wed, Thu & Sun*

Bob's Bar

24 C3

This lounge bar at the opulent Capella hotel offers knockout beverages and views of the resort's tranquil pools stretching towards the sea. *3-11pm Mon & Tue, from noon Wed-Sun*

Panamericana

25 D4

A clifftop grill restaurant serving a mixture of cuisines found along the Pan-American Hwy complemented with tantalising tipples. *noon-3pm & 5-9.15pm Mon-Thu, to 9.45pm Fri, noon-4pm & 5-9.45pm Sat, to 9.15pm Sun*

Elegant Sips

Pineapple Room

26 C3

Celebrate stately elegance from the yesteryears here with playful nods to the prickly fruit. Be spirited away by the curated cocktails. *5.30-11pm*

Chairman's Room

27 D3

An ethereal transient haven in Raffles Sentosa hotel featuring calligraphy and chinoiserie. The tart Sentosa Sling here beats the original in our humble opinion. *9am-11pm*

Shopping

Island Retailing

Weave

28 B1

Resorts World Sentosa's newest shopping enclave is a biophilic village with lifestyle shopping and dining options. *10am-10pm*

Resorts World Sentosa

29 B2

A luxurious shopping adventure, with many high-end stores, awaits at Resorts World Sentosa. Whether browsing or ready for a lavish splurge, prepare your credit cards. *10am-10pm*

Singapore Toolkit

Buddha Tooth Relic Temple (p62), Chinatown
VADIM_N/SHUTTERSTOCK

Family Travel

Travelling around Singapore with little ones in tow is a breeze – the city is safe, clean and super-efficient. Kids are welcome everywhere, and there are facilities and amenities catering to children of all ages.

Getting Around

Children under 90cm travel free on trains and buses with a paying adult. All MRT stations have lifts; pushchair users should follow blue Priority Use signs for safe routes. Prams are allowed on buses with designated restraint spaces. Rideshare service Grab offers family options with car restraints, bookable via the app.

LOCAL LOWDOWN

For the lowdown on Singapore's top attractions, kid-centric activities and family-friendly spots to make your trip unforgettable, check out SassyMama. **Scan the QR code for the latest tips:**

Feeding Little Tykes

Baby formula and food are found in supermarkets, although the available brands may differ from those at home. While many restaurants offer children's menus, it's advisable to request 'not spicy' options at hawker stalls. Simple dishes like chicken rice (pictured) are excellent choices for young children. Cut fruits are safe for consumption; juices are perfect for beating the heat.

Keeping Cool

Many outdoor parks, attractions and malls have free water-play areas for children; pack swimming gear, a hat and sun protection.

Discounted Tickets

Children enjoy discounted or free admission to many attractions. Student IDs are valid for discounted entry at many places.

Facilities

Shopping malls and many restaurants are equipped with changing facilities and child-friendly restrooms. While public breastfeeding is less common due to cultural norms, attitudes are evolving. Pavements are pram-friendly and cots are available at most hotels.

GOWITHSTOCK/SHUTTERSTOCK

Accommodation

Singapore offers anything from luxury hotels and heritage stays to midrange accommodation and hostels. Prices are fairly high.

Where to Stay if You Love...

Architecture, History & Knock-out Vistas

Downtown & Marina Bay (p35) Flush with showcase museums and a mix of striking old-school and modern architecture. Unsurprisingly pricey – but worth the splurge for the view.

We Love to Stay in...

Chinatown & the CBD (p59)
While the area around the pedestrianised shopping streets of Chinatown may feel overly touristy to some (although you'll find plenty of historical sites and some great hostels here), the enclaves beyond are peppered with top-notch cocktail bars, boutique hotels and some of the city's hottest restaurants.

Designer Stores & Mega Malls

Orchard Road (p101)
Singapore's world-famous shopping strip littered with high-end hotels and a smattering of oh-so-trendy slumber pads, but not much for budget travellers.

HOW MUCH FOR A NIGHT IN

Hostel dorm bed
from S$30

Midrange hotel
from S$300

Luxury abode
from S$600

Street Art, Boutiques & Shrines

Little India & Kampong Glam (p79) Central location with plenty of cheap accommodation and a smattering of higher-end boutiques and modern hotels. Streets can get very noisy, especially at weekends.

Peranakan Perfection & Cool Cafes

Eastern Singapore (p123) Breezy, laid-back neighbourhood vibes in the heartland of Peranakan culture. Affordable lodging and the MRT station means a quick zip into the city.

Adrenaline Thrills & Beachside Chills

Sentosa Island (p163) Singapore's island of fun is peppered with resort-style hotels, kid-friendly attractions, adrenaline-pumping amusements parks and chilled-out beach clubs.

Food, Drink & Nightlife

Allergies & Intolerances

People with food allergies and intolerances may face a few issues in Singapore but are generally well catered for. Restaurants and cafes usually list ingredients on menus; however, always ask your server to be sure. Hawker centres can be harder to navigate, as there can be a language barrier, and allergies are uncommon in the local population. Carry your medication with you.

INK N PROPELLER/SHUTTERSTOCK

MENU DECODER

Ayam – Chicken
Popiah – Spring roll with paper-like skin
Sambal – Spicy condiment
Congee – Rice porridge
Mian – Noodles
Murtabak – Indian stuffed pancake
Roti Prata – South Indian flatbread (pictured)
Laksa – Coconut-based noodle soup

HAPPY HOURS

Drinking here is expensive, but affordable tipples are still available. Hawker centres offer cheap beers, while many bars have happy-hour specials starting anytime from noon and lasting until 9pm. Deals range from two-for-one or discounted 'house pours', making it easier to enjoy a night out without breaking the bank.

Chope!

In hawker centres and food halls, it is customary to *chope* (save) a seat first, especially if it's busy, before ordering your food. Traditionally, this is done by laying a packet of tissues on each spot, but you'll also see people using umbrellas, business cards or even mobile phones.

HOW TO... Pay the Bill

Tipping Tipping is not common practice. Instead, most restaurants include a 10% service charge on the bill, and tipping is not expected at hawker centres.

Splitting the bill Generally, bills are split evenly, but it's okay to ask to pay a specific amount per card. Some restaurants have rules on how many cards they will split between – ask before dining.

Cash or card Cash is king at hawker centres, though many will accept local bank cards. Some cafes and restaurants are going cashless, and this is usually well signed.

PRICE RANGES

The following price ranges refer to the average cost of a main course.

$ less than S$15

$$ S$15-40

$$$ more than S$40

OPENING HOURS

Restaurants Noon to 2.30pm and 6pm to 11pm

Cafes 8am to 6pm

Hawker centres 7am to 10pm, some stalls until sold out

Going Out

Cocktail scene

Singapore has evolved into a global mixology hub. In classic establishments, rooftop bars and secret speakeasies, bartenders are experimenting with exotic ingredients and innovative techniques. Try **Live Twice**, **No Sleep Club** and **Native** in Chinatown (p76), **Backdrop** on Orchard Rd (p108) or Downtown's **Nutmeg & Clove** (p56).

When to go Bars generally open around 5pm until at least midnight Sunday to Thursday, and to 2am or 3am on Friday and Saturday.

At the door There may be a queue at some of the hottest bars, but door staff usually take your phone number and call when a spot becomes available.

Singapore Sling Created by Raffles Hotel barman Ngiam Tong Boon, the cocktail (pictured) first hit the bar in 1915. The recipe, once a tightly held secret, has long since been out and now many Singapore bars peddle a modern (read: more palatable) twist on the original.

HOW MUCH FOR A

Kopi (coffee)
S$1.40

Hawker meal
S$4–7

Beer at a hawker stall
S$8 per 750mL bottle

Glass of wine at a bar
S$18–30

Cocktail at a bar
S$25–40

Meal at a restaurant
S$25–45

Fine-dining dinner
S$150–500

SVETLANASF/SHUTTERSTOCK

LGBTIQ+ Travellers

Singapore is conservative, but there's increasing support for LGBTIQ+ rights. In 2022, the controversial 377A law that banned sex between two men was repealed.

Pink with a Purpose

Singapore's Pink Fest and Pink Dot SG are held each June to coincide with global Pride Month.

Pink Dot SG, a one-day festival established in 2009, is a celebration designed to bring LGBTIQ+ Singaporeans closer to their family and friends. Due to government regulations, only Singaporean citizens and permanent residents are allowed entry into the festival grounds.

The fringe event **Pink Fest** holds plenty of fun events – such as film screenings, fashion shows, a career fair and shopping market – for diverse audiences and everyone is welcome. Growing annually, these festivals symbolise pride with the colour pink – mirroring Singapore's identity-card colour – and are a mix of red and white, the colours of the national flag.

OUR PICK

Chinatown

The bulk of Singapore's LGBTIQ+ bars are clustered in Chinatown, home to long-time favourites as well as fresh faces such as **Restroom Bar** and **Carnival Haus** (p76), all on Neil Rd. For more nightlife fun, head to cocktail spot **Slippery Slope** (p76) or dance the night away at **Sweat Club** (p77).

A SAFE STAY

There's no specific LGBTIQ+ accommodation, but most hotels are LGBTIQ+ friendly. Several higher-end hostels offer private rooms or pods.

NINA NIN/SHUTTERSTOCK

WALK TO INCLUSIVITY

Join tour guide Isaac Tng as he walks you through Singapore's journey towards an inclusive nation.

Resources

- **hyper.com.sg** Epic parties organised for the queer community.
- **linktr.ee/proutapp** A safe virtual space for the Singapore LGBTIQ+ crew to connect and find queer-run and queer-inclusive meetups, resources and helplines.
- **oogachaga.com** Community-based organisation working with LGBTQ+ individuals, couples and families.

CLEARER SKIES

From 2026, Singapore has required departing airlines to use sustainable aviation fuel (SAF), reducing carbon emissions. The country aims for a 1% SAF target from 2026 and plans to raise it to 3–5% by 2030.

Shop Mindfully

Bypass the garish tourist tat, which is usually manufactured overseas, and instead seek out local artisans and eco-friendly and fair-trade products. The **Social Space**, is a socially conscious multiconcept store featuring cafes and fair-trade shopping. Singaporean label **Sandbar Swimwear** produces eco-beach gear from recycled plastic bottles, with each piece purchased funding the removal of 1kg of ocean plastic. For pre-loved apparel, explore Orchard Rd's **Lucky Plaza** where, on the upper floors, you'll find plenty of secondhand stores with bargains galore to sift through.

HIGH-SPEED CLEAN

Unleash your ecofriendly speed demon as you race at **HyperDrive**, Sentosa's electrifying go-kart circuit, knowing each kart leaves zero tailpipe emissions in its wake. Scan the QR code to book.

Climate Change & Travel

It's impossible to ignore the impact we have when travelling; Lonely Planet urges all travellers to engage with their travel carbon footprint, which will mainly come from air travel. While there often isn't an alternative, travellers can look to minimise the number of flights they take and use cleaner ground transport, such as trains. One proposed solution – purchasing carbon offsets – unfortunately does not cancel out the impact of individual flights. While most destinations will depend on air travel for the foreseeable future, for now, pursuing ground-based travel where possible is the best course of action.

The **UN Carbon Offset Calculator** shows how flying impacts a household's emissions.

The **ICAO's carbon emissions calculator** allows visitors to analyse the CO2 generated by point-to-point journeys.

Accessible Travel

Public Transport

All of Singapore's trains and buses are accessible. MRT stations are equipped with priority lifts, tactile wayfinding, easy-to-follow signage, visual and audible indicators, and wheelchair-accessible toilets. Buses have rear-door ramps (the bus captain will assist you in boarding), and designated wheelchair spaces and reserved seating. Almost all stops are barrier-free.

Taxis & Rideshare

There's no taxi surcharge for wheelchairs, but usually only smaller, foldable ones can fit in the boot. Rideshare app Grab offers wheelchair-accessible vehicles, ranging from ramp-equipped cars to those with ample storage for assistive devices.

FOR HIRE

Most main attractions offer free wheelchairs on a first come, first served basis. **AGIS Medical** *(agis.com.sg)* has mobility scooters and wheelchairs for daily hire, with delivery and collection available.

Accommodation

Many larger modern hotels in Singapore are equipped with facilities such as accessible rooms and bathrooms, but older-style shophouse and hostel accommodation often is not. Call ahead to discuss your requirements.

OUR PICK

Explore the nation's story with inclusivity at the **National Museum of Singapore**. The entire facility, including galleries, is wheelchair-accessible, and free wheelchairs are offered at the Visitor Services counter. For details about Quiet Mornings, Quiet Corners, a dedicated sensory room and the availability of sensory bags and visual schedules, see nhb.gov.sg/nationalmuseum.

CROWDED PLACES

Although most of Singapore has good wheelchair access, Chinatown and Little India have narrow and crowded footpaths, which can be a challenge for anyone with mobility, sight or hearing issues.

Resources

- **visitsingapore.com/travel-tips/essential-travel-information** The Visit Singapore tourist office provides information on navigating Singapore's modes of transport and built environment with ease.

Nuts & Bolts

Opening Hours

In Singapore, hours are consistent year-round but hawker stalls close once they've sold out.

Banks 8.30am to 4.30pm Monday to Friday, 9.30am to noon Saturday

Restaurants Noon to 2.30pm and 6pm to 11pm

Hawker centres, food courts and coffee shops 7am to 10pm

Bars 3pm to 1am

Clubs 10pm to 3am or 6am

Malls 10am to 9pm

Wet markets 6am to noon, larger markets to 5pm

The metric system is used in Singapore.

QUICK INFO

Time zone Singapore Standard Time (GMT/UTC plus eight hours)

Country code +65

Emergency number 995

Population 6.04 million

ELECTRICITY

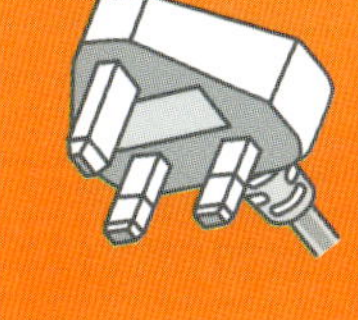

Type G
230V/50Hz

Smoking

Smoking is prohibited practically everywhere in Singapore, including parks, beaches and bus stops with fines of up to S$500. Designated smoking points are the only allowed areas. E-cigarettes and vapes are illegal. There are no duty-free concessions or Goods and Services Tax (GST) relief. Cigarettes must be declared at Customs.

Public Holidays

Most malls, shops, attractions, museums and restaurants remain open on public holidays, except for the two-day holiday for Chinese New Year when virtually all shops close. The Istana, the official residence and office of the president of Singapore, opens its grounds on numerous public holidays – see istana.gov.sg for details.

New Year's Day 1 January

Chinese New Year Two days in January/February

Good Friday March/April

Hari Raya Puasa (Eid al-Fitr) Feb/March

Hari Raya Haji April/May

Labour Day 1 May

Vesak Day May

National Day 9 August

Deepavali October/November

Christmas Day 25 December

Index

Sights p000 Map pages **p000**

See also separate subindexes for:

Eating p189

Drinking p190

Shopping p191

Eating

Drinking

Shopping

Send Us Your Feedback

We love to hear from travellers – your comments help make our books better. We read every word, and we guarantee that your feedback goes straight to the authors. Visit lonelyplanet.com/contact to submit your updates and suggestions.

Note: We may edit, reproduce and incorporate your comments in Lonely Planet products such as guidebooks, websites and digital products, so let us know if you are happy to have your name acknowledged. For a copy of our privacy policy visit lonelyplanet.com/legal.

Acknowledgements

Cover photograph: Peranakan terrace houses, Koon Seng Rd. Nabina Nazar/Kintzing

Back photograph: Giant panda, Mandai Wildlife Reserve (p142). Shazwany/Shutterstock

THIS BOOK

The 9th edition of Lonely Planet's *Pocket Singapore* guidebook was researched and written by Ria de Jong, Jaclynn Seah and Morgan Awyong. The previous edition was written by Ria de Jong. This guidebook was produced by the following:

Destination Editor
James Pham

Coordinating Editor
Mani Ramaswamy

Cartographer
Anthony Phelan

Production Editor
Barbara Delissen

Image Researcher
Zac Tan

Cover Researcher
Giada de Agostinis

Thanks to
Melanie Dankel, Kate James, Kellie Langdon, Jenna Myers, Fionnuala Twomey

Published by Lonely Planet Global Limited
CRN 554153
9th edition – Aug 2026
ISBN 978 1 83869 918 5

10 9 8 7 6 5 4 3 2 1
Printed in China